Finding Help
for
Struggling Teens

A GUIDE FOR PARENTS AND THE
PROFESSIONALS WHO WORK WITH THEM

Frederic G. Reamer and Deborah H. Siegel

NASW PRESS
National Association of Social Workers
Washington, DC

Elvira Craig de Silva, DSW, ACSW, President
Elizabeth J. Clark, PhD, ACSW, MPH, Executive Director

Cheryl Y. Bradley, *Publisher*
Schandale Kornegay, *Manager, Publications*
Marcia Roman, *Managing Editor, Journals and Books*
Caroline Polk, *Copy Editor*
Sarah Lowman, *Proofreader*
Bernice Eisen, *Indexer*

Cover design by Larnish & Associates, Vienna, VA
Interior design by MidAtlantic Books & Journals, Inc., Baltimore, MD
Printed by Victor Graphics, Inc., Baltimore, MD

Library of Congress Cataloging-in-Publication Data

Reamer, Frederic G., 1953-
  Finding help for struggling teens : a guide for parents and the professionals who work with them / by Frederic G. Reamer and Deborah H. Siegel.
    p.   cm.
  Includes index.
  ISBN-13: 978-0-87101-373-6
  ISBN-10: 0-87101-373-8
    1. Teenagers—Services for—United States. 2. Problem youth—Services for—United States.
I. Siegel, Deborah H., 1951- II. Title.
HV1431.R4195 2006
362.7083'0973—dc22

                                                                                          2006015647

Published in the United States

For Emma and Leah

Contents

Acknowledgments

We would like to recognize a remarkable group of professionals who have devoted their careers to struggling teens. We have been inspired and influenced by their extraordinary insight, knowledge, competence, wisdom, commitment, vision, focus on strengths, faith, and hope. Special thanks to Brad Bannon, Sara Beck, Charlotte Blend, Gus Buchanan, Kathy Butts, Kevin Douglas, Christian Dymond, Stan Eddy, Lonnie Edson, Molly Huddle, David Kammerer, Isaiah Keepin, Linda Koulouris, Hillary Kramer, Leslie Moulin, Collin O'Leary, Kathy Rossman, John Rouleau, Jessica Scriver, Emily Skoler, C. J. Spirito, Kelly Story, Jean Waltz, and, especially, Ryan Weiland. These people change lives.

CHAPTER 1

Struggling Teens:

ISSUES AND CHALLENGES

The adolescent years can be challenging. Although adolescence can be an emotionally stormy phase for virtually all teenagers, sometimes a youth's struggles are especially intense and require intervention. Many teens struggle with issues related to mental health, family relationships, friends, school performance, substance abuse, sexuality, and various high-risk behaviors. For example:

▲ Amanda, 15, lived with her parents and younger brother. Amanda was a bright child but struggled academically. She had a learning disability and had been diagnosed with attention deficit/hyperactivity disorder (ADHD) in the second grade. Often she had difficulty making friends and felt like she did not "fit in." Amanda's parents had adopted her at birth and were aware of her birth family's long history of mental health struggles. Amanda's parents accessed counseling for themselves and Amanda throughout her childhood to get extra support and help her develop coping skills. They knew Amanda had low self-esteem despite all their efforts to help her feel good about herself.

Amanda began hanging out with several teens she met on the Internet via instant messaging and, before long, was skipping school with them, experimenting with drugs, and refusing to be home by her 10 p.m. curfew. Amanda, always a feisty child, began to argue with her parents constantly and refused to obey basic family rules. Amanda's parents feared for her safety, could no longer tolerate her rebellious behavior, and felt desperate to find help.

▲ Stan, 17, was arrested by the police for cocaine possession. He had been using cocaine and marijuana for several months. Stan sold drugs to friends so he would have money to support his own heavy drug use, which had started shortly after his parents divorced and his father remarried. Stan's parents sent him to an after-school teen substance abuse program in their community, and the whole family attended several counseling sessions there, but Stan's drug use and defiant behavior continued. Stan kept slipping out of school during the day; occasionally snuck out of bed in the middle of the night to talk on the phone and use the computer; had failing grades; and was chronically combative, hostile, and oppositional. Stan's parents became afraid of him. They did not know what to do to stop his downward slide.

The lawyer handling Stan's drug charges told his mother that she, with the lawyer's help, should try to find a therapeutic boarding school for Stan. The lawyer explained that a judge might be willing to order Stan to the school as an alternative to sentencing him to a juvenile correctional facility.

▲ Tamar got along well with her parents and siblings and was a strong student until age 16, when she became sullen and withdrawn. Her grades slipped and, on several occasions, she cut her arms with a blade and burned the backs of her hands with cigarettes. Tamar's school social worker referred her to a psychiatrist, who began treating her for depression. After two suicidal gestures, Tamar's psychiatrist suggested that Tamar's parents find a residential treatment center that could help with her mental health and school issues. Unfortunately, Tamar's parents were unemployed and did not have comprehensive health care coverage to pay for the services Tamar needed.

▲ Dwayne, 16, lived with his grandmother. Dwayne's mother died of a drug overdose when he was eight years old; he never met his father. Dwayne was suspended from school after fighting with another student who attacked Dwayne for being "a black fag." Dwayne had wondered for years about his sexual orientation, and he had experienced sexual relations with several teenage boys and older men. He dreaded going to school because he felt so unsafe there; he was picked on and tormented relentlessly by peers while teachers and school staff remained silent and failed to intervene. Dwayne's grand-mother worried about his failing grades, moodiness, and despair; she knew he needed help but did not know where to turn. Dwayne tried outpatient counseling at the local mental health center, but he remained chronically distraught and overwrought. Dwayne's grand-mother was frightened by his agitation, angry outbursts, and moodi-ness.

In each example, the parents and guardians—like the parents and guardians of struggling teens everywhere—did their best to raise happy, well-adjusted children who felt loved and secure.[1] From infancy, they talked to their children, showed them love, gave them consistent discipline, said bedtime prayers, read to them, monitored how much television they watched and with whom they played, went to parent–teacher meetings on open school nights, read parenting books, talked with other parents for problem-solving ideas, and asked their pediatricians for advice. When things got tough, these parents attended meetings with school staff and administrators, had their children evaluated to determine whether they had special needs, arranged for their children to receive mental health counsel-ing, agreed to have their children try medications their psychiatrist recom-mended, went to family therapy and marriage counseling to improve com-munication and parenting skills, enrolled their children in outpatient substance abuse counseling programs, admitted their children to inpatient psychiatric facilities, lost sleep, cried, and prayed. These parents received so much advice—some consistent and some contradictory—that their heads began to spin: "Be firmer!" "Don't be so rigid and demanding!" "Be gentler." "Stand your ground!" "Try to listen and be more supportive." No wonder these parents felt uncertain, confused, off balance, blamed—and raw.

Parents of struggling teens can find and receive help. Over time, strug-gling teens and their families can make great progress, although the road can be long and hard. The key challenge, for many, is knowing where to begin and what to do next—where to turn in times of crisis. When crises emerge, most parents of struggling teens scramble frantically for information

---

1. Not all struggling teens live with their parents. Some parents struggle with their own mental health, substance abuse, financial, legal, and other problems. In such cases, the teen might live with grandparents, friends, other relatives, in foster homes, or group homes. To avoid cumbersome terminology, throughout this book the term "parents" also includes other guardians of struggling teens.

and assistance, grasping for help that turns out to be fragmented and unco-ordinated. This book is for them.

This guide is designed to provide parents of struggling teens, as well as the professionals who work with them, with a concise overview of issues they are likely to face, the range of available services and programs, practical strategies for finding the right services and programs, and advice about how to cope with a struggling teen.

Who Is a Struggling Teen? Warning Signs

The term *struggling teen* describes youths who show signs of distress, some subtle and some obvious. Common warning signs include the following behaviors:

- ▲ Isolation and withdrawal: Most teens withdraw from parents, but some sink into themselves too far. They may feel profoundly alone and alienated, unable to connect with any safe adult. They crave friendships but feel too demoralized and fearful to reach out to others or respond to friendly overtures. Many struggling teens have poor self-image and little confidence. They doubt that they can be competent and successful, and they become increasingly cut off from school, family, and friends. These teens are easy prey for involvement with "the wrong crowd" because of their hunger to belong.

- ▲ School failure and truancy: Many struggling teens perform poorly in school. Some were strong students in grade school but became discouraged and alienated from academics in middle school or high school. Other teens have difficulty with school their entire lives because of learning disabilities, mental health issues, difficult home lives, or school environments that are hostile, unresponsive, racist, and non-nurturing.

- ▲ Defiance toward authority: Many struggling teens refuse to obey rules laid down by parents, teachers, the police, and other authority figures. They may refuse to obey rules at home, cheat on school assignments, and become involved in delinquent activity (for example, shoplifting, reckless driving, and drug use). They may be suspended or expelled from school, chronically truant, or in trouble with the police.

▲ Running away from home: Teens may run away from home to escape conflict with their parents, assert their independence, avoid the consequences of breaking rules, or flee their own distressing emotions.

▲ Choosing the "wrong" friends: Teens normally seek solace from peers. Struggling teens have a knack for finding other struggling teens. These friends, who themselves are having a difficult time, engage the teen in high-risk behaviors, such as drug and alcohol use, sex, and delinquency.

▲ Impulsive behavior: Teens who hang out with other struggling teens sometimes engage in high-risk and impulsive behaviors such as speeding, shoplifting, using drugs and alcohol, and having unprotected sex. They may have a "devil-may-care" attitude and take chances because they feel invulnerable and believe they have everything under control. Teens who abuse drugs and alcohol are even more likely to engage in impulsive behavior because of their impaired judgment.

▲ Getting in trouble with the law: Struggling teens may break the law, ranging from committing crimes against property (for example, spray-painting graffiti, turning over gravestones, stealing cars) to committing violent crimes (for example, assault, robbery, rape).

▲ Depression: A significant percentage of struggling teens show signs of depression. Common symptoms include poor appetite or overeating; difficulty with sleep (insomnia, premature awakening, or sleeping too much); low energy and fatigue; low self-esteem; poor concentration; difficulty making decisions; feelings of hopelessness, guilt, and worthlessness; and irritability.

▲ Abusing alcohol or drugs: Many struggling teens experiment with or abuse alcohol or drugs, including marijuana, methamphetamines, cocaine, heroin, or medications. Teens who are abusing substances may experience a persistent desire for the substance; difficulty cutting down or controlling consumption despite negative consequences; frequent intoxication; withdrawal symptoms; impaired school, job, or social functioning; and a need for increased amounts of the substance to achieve a "high."

▲ Eating disorders: Some struggling teens show signs of an eating disorder, such as anorexia nervosa or bulimia. They may seriously undereat, binge eat, or purge through vomiting or laxative use. Teens can compulsively overeat or exercise excessively to avoid weight gain.

▲ Self-injury: Some teenagers try to hurt themselves by cutting, burning, branding, bruising, or hitting themselves, among other methods. Mental health professionals generally agree that teens who try to hurt themselves in these ways do so in an effort to cope with emotional pain; the self-injury temporarily releases unbearable psychological tension.

Teens in every community, from the most affluent to the poorest, encounter challenges during their adolescent years that can lead to trouble. Families in low-income, economically distressed communities face special challenges, including high rates of poverty and crime. Oppression and discrimination permeate their lives. Research shows that teens living in economically distressed communities are more likely to engage in high-risk activities, be unsupervised after school, and lack adequate health and mental health care.[2]

The challenges that typical adolescents face can be especially severe for low-income teens who are of color, immigrants, or refugees. Because of racism and prejudice, these youths' needs may be ignored. They may be singled out; bullied and taunted; victimized in racially charged incidents; and harassed by educators, local merchants, neighbors, or police who target teens of color, assume they are "trouble," and lack compassion for the challenges these youths face. Racial and ethnic tensions contribute to the behaviors that sometimes get these teens in trouble.

Fortunately, help is available.

---

2. For additional discussion of the unique challenges and risks faced by teens living in economically distressed communities, see Rolf Loeber and David P. Farrington, eds., *Child Delinquents: Development, Intervention, and Service Needs* (Thousand Oaks, CA: Sage Publications, 2001) and Gail A. Wasserman, Kate Keenan, Richard E. Tremblay, John D. Coie, Todd I. Herrenkohl, Rolf Loeber, and David Petechuk, "Risk and Protective Factors of Child Delinquency," Child Delinquent Bulletin Series, (Washington, DC: Office of Juvenile Justice and Delinquency Prevention, U.S. Department of Justice), April 2003, available at http://www.ncjrs.gov/html/ojjdp/193409/contents.html.

CHAPTER 2

Finding Services and Programs for Struggling Teens:

QUESTIONS TO ASK

Programs and services for struggling teens can be found in many ways. Parents can start by contacting school personnel (for example, guidance counselors, social workers, student adjustment counselors, administrators), community-based family service agencies, mental health centers, neighborhood centers, other social service programs designed specifically for at-risk youths and their families, public child welfare agencies, family and juvenile courts, specialty courts (such as truancy and drug courts), and clergy. Some communities provide structured programs that offer families comprehensive assessment, evaluation, information, referral, and case management. These programs help parents decide what kinds of help they need, where to find that help, and how to coordinate the various helpers' efforts.[1]

The professionals who work in these various settings can be helpful in different ways. Mental health providers (for example, clinical social workers, psychologists, counselors, psychiatric nurses, psychiatrists) can help parents and struggling teens improve their communication skills, resolve conflicts, learn how to understand one another better, and identify and address challenging mental health issues (for example, depression, anxiety, ADHD). It is important to choose a mental health provider who has at least a master's degree, a professional license, and experience with the issues

---

1. Parents can consult local child welfare and mental health professionals who work with adolescents to obtain the names of the social service agencies that sponsor these programs.

your family is facing. It is crucial that you feel comfortable with the mental health provider. Trust your gut. If a provider does not feel right to you, that person is not the best provider for you.

Educational advocates and *educational consultants* may be able to help parents and teens obtain needed school services. Educational advocates, who are often attorneys, help people obtain specialized educational services from the public school system. Educational advocates charge parents a fee and work with local, state, and federal education officials to ensure that students receive the services and "special accommodations" to which they are entitled by law. Advocates may file claims in court to force school districts to provide or pay for special-needs services and programs outside the school district. They may attend meetings at school to represent the parents' and teen's points of view when school personnel meet to develop an individualized education program (IEP) that addresses the struggling teen's special education needs.

Educational consultants help parents locate programs, services, and specialty schools designed to meet their child's needs. Educational consultants charge parents a fee; assess each teen's unique strengths and needs; and help the family find the most appropriate services, schools, or programs for their teen. Many educational consultants monitor the student's progress in the new program or school and, when necessary, advocate for the teen with that program or school when challenging issues arise.

Often parents do not have the money to purchase services from an educational advocate or consultant. On occasion, those services might be available through public or private child welfare agencies. For example, a social worker in a private family service agency where the family is receiving counseling may be willing to go with the parents to a child's IEP meeting at school to help the parents assert their points of view. Perhaps this private agency uses a sliding-fee scale or has a grant that provides this service free of charge. A social worker in a state public child welfare agency may be able to help parents by sharing his or her professional experience with schools and programs for struggling teens. Some communities have tax- or grant-funded programs that provide educational advocates to work with low-income parents who need support negotiating with schools to get their child's needs met.

Other parents who have been through similar experiences with their own children and have personal experience with IEP meetings may be able to provide informal help as educational advocates for other families. Sometimes, a veteran parent will attend IEP meetings with a family in need, offering a shoulder to lean on and another pro-child voice in the conversation.[2] Clergy, friends, even one of the teen's former teachers also could play this role. Sometimes parents feel intimidated, outnumbered, voiceless, overwhelmed, or disempowered in an IEP meeting. Having an "outsider" at their side may help parents more effectively present their points of view in the meeting and, later, process what was said during the meeting.

Parents need to know that, for financial reasons, school systems and agencies may be reluctant to agree to provide the services a child needs. Hence, parents and their advocates must be dogged in their insistence that needed services be provided. Parents, understandably, may become disheartened and angry when schools and agencies claim the child does not need a service that parents and other professionals are certain the child does need. An advocate can help parents argue their case and maneuver through bureaucratic obstacles more effectively.

Selecting the right educational consultant is vital. Competent and ethical educational consultants provide a thorough assessment and comprehensive information to help parents make wise choices. Some people who call themselves educational consultants, however, have little formal education and training. They may be biased in favor of certain kinds of programs and schools that might not be best for their clients.

Here is a list of questions to ask when selecting an educational consultant:

▲ How much experience does the educational consultant have?

▲ What is the educational consultant's educational and professional background? Does the consultant have at least a master's degree in a mental health field or in education? Does the educational consultant hold any professional licenses or certifications? If not, be wary.

▲ What services will the educational consultant provide?

▲ What are the full costs? Does the educational consultant charge by the hour or by the placement?

---

2. In many communities, the local Learning Disabilities Association (LDA) office may make available experienced parents of youths with learning differences and special needs to provide advocacy advice and support to other parents. Support from experienced parents also can be obtained from parenting networks found in many communities.

▲ Does the educational consultant have any formal ties to specific programs and schools (which may lead to biased referrals and conflicts of interest), or does the educational consultant provide unbiased information and advice?

▲ What does the educational consultant do to monitor the teen's progress during his or her enrollment in the program or school? How often does the consultant visit the program or school during the teen's stay?

▲ How much contact will the educational consultant have with the parents while the teen is in a program or school?

▲ Do you feel comfortable with and trust the educational consultant?

You can find educational advocates and educational consultants in several ways:

▲ Ask other parents. Spread the word among parents who have faced similar parenting challenges. Rely on parents whose judgment you respect and whose values and parenting philosophy match your own.

▲ Contact specialty organizations that focus on issues closely related to the teen's special needs. Organizations that focus on developmental disabilities and learning disorders may be able to recommend educational advocates and consultants. For example, Children and Adults with Attention-Deficit/Hyperactivity Disorder (CHADD) provides valuable information and referrals.

▲ To find educational advocates, contact the local bar association and ask for a list of attorneys who specialize in this kind of work. Before retaining an attorney to serve as an educational advocate, find out whether the attorney is

  • licensed to practice in your state

  • experienced in educational advocacy

- familiar with relevant education statutes and regulations

- sensitive to the teenager's and family's unique needs

- willing to attend IEP meetings at the teenager's school.

▲ To find educational consultants, consult listings provided by the Independent Educational Consultants Association (http://www.educationalconsulting.org/), which is a national organization whose members are full-time professionals.

What Kind of Help Does the Teen Need? Conducting an Assessment

To find the right services, school, or program for a struggling teen, it is important to have a good understanding of his or her unique challenges and needs. This information not only may help parents and professionals choose the right program or school, but also may be useful to staff at the program or school in which the teenager enrolls. In fact, one criterion for selecting a program or school is the admissions personnel's interest in all evaluation and assessment information available on your child and their willingness to tailor their educational, mental health, and other services to meet your child's unique needs.

A comprehensive assessment should include the following information about the teenager:

▲ Personal history

- Birth circumstances: What noteworthy events during the pregnancy may have affected the child, such as premature birth, prenatal drug exposure, or trauma during pregnancy or delivery?

- Developmental milestones: When did the teenager reach typical developmental milestones (for example, speech, social skills, fine and gross motor skills)?

- Strengths and supports: Who are the teenager's supports, such as caring and involved family members, friends, teachers, youth advisers, coaches, clergy, or other members of the community?

- Successful experiences: What successful experiences has the teenager had? What made those successes possible? When did they occur, and what were the circumstances?

- Ethnic heritage and considerations: What is the teenager's ethnic heritage? How comfortable with and proud of this heritage is the teen? What kinds of racism and discrimination has the teen experienced? How sensitive to ethnicity must the new school or program be?

- Religious heritage and considerations: What is the teenager's religious heritage? How comfortable is the teen with this heritage? What kind of religious discrimination has the teen experienced? What kind of religious programs and supports does the teenager need in the new school or program?

- Temperament: To what extent has the teenager always had predictable reactions to everyday situations (for example, shyness, impulsivity, irritability, oppositionality, low frustration tolerance, difficulties making transitions, inflexibility, explosiveness)?

- Social relationships: How well has the teen made and kept friends? What are the friendships like? How many friends does the child typically have? How long do those relationships last? How well does the teenager get along with friends?

- Mental status: What is the teenager's history with respect to moods, thoughts and perceptions, and cognitive functioning? With which mental health issues, if any, has the teen been diagnosed? For example, does the teen have anxiety, depression, obsessive–compulsive disorder, posttraumatic stress disorder, bipolar disorder, oppositional defiant disorder, Asperger syndrome, a pervasive developmental disorder, sensory integration dysfunction, or adjustment reactions?

- Stressors: What are the stressors in the teenager's life (for example, parents' divorce, chronic unemployment, frequent moves and changes in school, loss of loved ones, family violence, learning disability, poverty, traumatic brain injury, chronic illness)?

- Past and current problems: What have been the most significant problems in the teenager's life (for example, emotional, behavioral, educational, medical, social)?

- What are the symptoms?

- How severe have the problems been?

- How long has the teen struggled with the problems?

- When have these problems not been present or been less severe?

• Past efforts to address problems

- Services and programs: What mental health, educational, and other social services has the teenager received (for example, psychiatric hospitalization, outpatient counseling, tutoring, substance abuse treatment)?

- Effectiveness: Which of these services and programs have been most and least helpful?

• Education issues: What have been the teenager's successes in school? What challenges has the teen faced in school? Has the teen been formally evaluated for learning disabilities? Does the teen have a "504 plan" (that is, a legal document that specifies a program of services to help students with special needs in a regular education setting) or an IEP (a written plan for a child who has been diagnosed by a team of professionals as having disabilities that require special education services)? If so, what are the IEP components?

• Employment/vocational history: What paid or volunteer jobs has the teenager held? How successful were these experiences? What kinds of structures or supports enhance the teen's likelihood of success?

• Legal issues: What legal risks has the teenager taken (for example, driving under the influence, reckless driving, drug possession, truancy, shoplifting)? What legal charges have been filed? Has the teenager been placed on probation or incarcerated?

▲ Family history

• Familial and other significant relationships: What is the teenager's current family situation? Who lives in the home with the teenager? With what family members does the teenager have positive or conflictual relationships? How do family members get along with one another? What kinship resources are available to the teenager?

- Changes in family: What family members has the teen lost as a result of divorce, separation, foster care, adoption, or death? What family members have been added to the family as a result of remarriage or adoption? How have these losses and additions been addressed in the family?

- Family mental health and substance abuse history: What is the family's history of mental health issues, substance abuse issues, alcoholism, sexual abuse, physical abuse, or neglect? What diagnoses appear on the family tree?

- Medical history: What illnesses and physical disabilities in the family have affected the teen?

- Financial issues: How adequate has the family's income been? To what extent have poverty and unemployment been part of the family's history?

▲ Teenager's understanding of his or her current circumstances

- What is the teenager's definition of the problems she or he faces? To what does the teen attribute the problems? What are the teen's ideas about solutions? To what extent does the teen take responsibility for choices and behavior? How much insight does the teen have?

- How motivated does the teenager appear to be to address challenges?

- What kind of help does the teen want?

▲ Parents' and other key family members' understanding of the teenager's current circumstances

- How do the teenager's parents and other important people in the teen's life understand his or her current challenges? What do they think has led to the teen's current situation?

- What strengths, skills, and resources does the teen's family have that have helped them cope with the challenges of a struggling teen?

- How ready do the teenager's parents and other important people in the teen's life feel to address the issues and be part of interventions, services, and treatments?

- What do they think would be most helpful to them and the teenager?

How Do We Select the Right Program or School? Questions to Ask

Parents (and their advisers) must thoroughly examine schools and programs before deciding which is likely to be most appropriate. Parents should not select a school or program on the basis of reputations, glossy brochures, videos, Web site information, or word of mouth. Parents need to look deep beneath the surface and probe for detailed information from multiple, informed sources. Hasty, impulsive choices can backfire and lead to more disruption and distress. Parents should ask the following questions:

▲ How big is the school or program? Small schools and programs generally can provide more personalized, individualized attention and close supervision and monitoring. In large schools and programs, it may be easy for teenagers to "fly below the radar" and get lost in the crowd. For those reasons, some programs (for example, wilderness therapy programs) immediately place teenagers into small groups for their entire stay. Hence, the total number of teenagers in a program may not be as important as the amount and quality of attention the teenager receives from consistent caregivers who spend time with the teen and truly know, understand, and have a positive working relationship with the teen.

▲ Is the program accredited and licensed? Accreditation agencies typically require schools and programs to undergo a thorough review that includes site visits, interviews with teenagers and staff, and examination of school and program policies, programs, documents, and records. The goal of the accreditation process is to ensure that programs and schools meet standards related to admission procedures, services provided, staffing, health and safety, facilities, governance and administration, and finances. Accreditation does not guarantee that programs and schools are of high quality, but it does demonstrate that programs and schools are willing to undergo outside review and scrutiny and attempt to meet standards. Unfortunately, even an accredited program may be of questionable quality, so parents need to ask other questions as well.

Various organizations, including those on the list that follows, accredit programs and schools for struggling teens:

- Commission on Accreditation of Rehabilitation Facilities (CARF): CARF accredits alcohol and substance abuse treatment programs; child and youth services programs; mental health and behavioral health programs; and supported-living programs.

- The Joint Commission on Accreditation of Healthcare Organizations (JCAHO): JCAHO accredits a wide range of health care organizations, including behavioral health programs that serve struggling teens.

- The Council on Accreditation (COA): COA accredits organizations that provide community-based and residential services such as alcohol and chemical dependency counseling; case management; supported and independent living; individual and family counseling; and day treatment.

- Regional accreditation agencies for independent schools: In the United States, educational institutions—including boarding schools that serve struggling teens—are accredited by regional rather than national organizations. Examples of prominent regional organizations are the Independent Schools Association of the Central States; Independent Schools Association of the Southwest; Middle States Association of Colleges and Schools; New England Association of Schools and Colleges; North Central Association of Colleges and Schools; Pacific Northwest Association of Independent Schools; Southern Association of Colleges and Schools; and the Western Association of Schools and Colleges.

▲ What are the credentials and experience of the staff? Parents should assess the extent to which the teaching, clinical, and health care staff have appropriate education, training, credentials, and experience. Some schools and programs lack strict hiring criteria for teachers and other staff. For example, unprofessional and unscrupulous schools and programs may assign classroom instructors and other staff without graduate degrees in mental health professions to supervise seminars that mimic group therapy; those experiences can be destructively confrontational, emotionally abusive, and model destructive or dysfunctional communication styles and poor problem-solving skills.

▲ How well are staff supervised? How does the administration handle staff misbehavior and unprofessional conduct? If a staff member makes a mistake (for example, curses at a teen, touches a teen inappropriately, is stopped by the police for driving under the influence), what are the program's procedures and written policies for addressing the conduct? Are parents informed when such issues arise?

▲ To what extent does the program or school tailor services to meet each teenager's unique needs? Some schools and programs wisely offer specialized services (for example, counseling, education, behavior management) tailored to each teenager's individual needs. Other schools and programs, however, take more of a "one-size-fits-all" approach and use a single model with every youth. Such programs may assume a doctrinaire approach, one based on a firm belief that a particular model is best for everyone. Staff of those programs discourage any criticism or critical questions parents or others may ask. If the model is not working, staff claim that it is because of the teen's or parents' "bad attitude" or lack of cooperation.

▲ How much structure does the program or school provide? Ask about the daily and weekend schedules. Are afternoons and evenings filled with meaningful, supervised activities, or do teenagers spend excessive amounts of time "hanging out" without skilled supervision?

▲ How clearly laid out in writing are the program's or school's rules and disciplinary procedures? How readily does the program or school share those written policies with parents of prospective students and clients?

▲ Does the program or school take a nonpunitive and compassionate approach to discipline? Do staff routinely label, judge, and blame (for example, "You're a quitter, drama queen, manipulator, and lazy.")

when teens misbehave, or do they handle misbehavior construc-
tively and firmly, without shaming, and treat the situation as a learning and growth opportunity? To what extent do staff understand that
a teen's misbehavior can stem from lack of skills and insight, information-processing issues, immature frontal lobe development, emotional distress, a learning disability, or problems with the medication
the teenager takes for mental health issues? Do staff intervene to
address the underlying issues while doling out reasonable consequences? Do staff focus on each teenager's unique strengths, or do
they tend to blame, condemn, and judge teenagers who struggle?

▲ In what ways does the program or school involve parents and family? Many parents and family members are eager to be involved in
the teenager's care.[3] Some programs and schools stay in close touch
with parents and guardians by offering periodic updates by telephone or e-mail, consulting when issues or crises arise, sponsoring
group meetings with family members and students, and meeting in
person for staff–parent conferences. How often do staff communicate
with parents and family? Is a staff member always present when a
teen is allowed to call home? If so, the teen may not feel free to speak
candidly with parents about problems at the school or program.

▲ How sensitive is the program or school to the teenager's ethnicity, culture, and religion? What programs and supports does the program or
school offer to support cultural and religious practices? Some teens
who are members of ethnic, cultural, or religious minority groups may
not feel comfortable in programs and schools where most of the other
teenagers are of a different group. Teenagers who feel out of place may
find it hard to adjust to schools and programs and may not benefit fully
from available services. Parents and others must be sensitive to the
challenges that teenagers who are members of minority groups may
face and explore whether particular schools and programs are suffi-
ciently sensitive and responsive to diversity issues.

---

3. The term "family" here is used flexibly and openly to include not only those who are
related to the teen by blood or law but also those who are related by love and affection, such
as close friends, neighbors, teachers, religious leaders, godparents, stepparents, and others.
A teen's "kinship community" includes any adult who might provide this teenager with
nurture and protection.

▲ How sensitive is the program or school to the teenager's sexual orientation? What programs and supports does the program or school offer to support the teenager's sexual orientation?

▲ How does the program or school handle teenagers' mental health and psychotropic medication needs? How readily do staff recognize that teenagers' struggles sometimes are a result of their mental health challenges (for example, clinical depression, bipolar disorder, eating disorder, anxiety)? Before admissions and upon intake, do staff ask parents for detailed written information about the teenager's mental health history and treatment? How, if at all, is that information taken into account in designing an individualized package of services for the teenager and when staff respond to challenges and crises that arise in the teenager's life? Are staff willing to administer psychotropic medication at the times recommended by the teenager's physician, rather than at times that are convenient for the program or school staff? Some programs and schools will not tailor their medication schedules to meet teenagers' unique needs and physician instructions. As a result of this medication mismanagement, teenagers may have difficulty complying with instructions and expectations, possibly leading to noncompliant or inappropriate behavior that results in discipline.

▲ What is the program or school's attrition rate? Most programs and schools expect some attrition, as a result of the nature of the population they serve, but some have unusually high attrition rates. Heavy attrition may be a red flag. Stable, reputable programs and schools tend to have relatively low attrition rates. High turnover in a program or a low graduation rate in a school may be a sign of turmoil, instability, a punitive environment, teens who "melt down" in a hostile and non-nurturing setting, or disgruntled parents. Parents who are unhappy or disenchanted with a program are more likely to withdraw their child, leading to high attrition.

▲ How often do teenagers run away from the program or school? Struggling teenagers need a program or school that has constructive methods for helping them develop the ability to comply with rules and expectations. High rates of teenagers running away from a program or school may be evidence of the program's or school's ineffective or punitive methods.

The Most Common Mistakes to Avoid
When Selecting a Program or School

Parents of a struggling teen sometimes feel lost and desperate with fear, frustration, and anger. They may feel torn between their undying love for their troubled child and their outrage over the child's misbehavior. Parents may want to flee or hang in there, hoping that what has not worked in the past will finally show positive results. Slowly they come to realize that different, new interventions are needed. Of one thing these parents are sure: Something must change, and quickly, before their child is irreparably hurt. In some instances, the teenager's challenging behaviors have escalated over time; in other cases a sudden crisis necessitates immediate placement in a program or school. In either case, parents feel intense pressure to immediately stop their teen from spinning out of control.

Despite the pressures to act decisively and immediately, it is important to avoid several common mistakes in choosing a program or school.

Picking a Program Quickly and Impulsively

A program should be selected only after careful consultation and exploration. Hundreds of specialty programs and schools for students are out there. It is difficult for parents to have enough inside information about each one to be able to choose the best match for their child. Although it can be extremely expensive to consult an informed professional (for example, therapist, educational advocate, educational consultant) who has visited the program or school, has experience with it over time, and has direct feedback from other parents who enrolled their children in the program or school, in the long run it is wise to do so.

Sometimes a consultant may recommend a program or school about which the parents have important reservations. Parents must trust their own instincts and judgment and value their own opinions when making decisions about their child. Hence, in addition to obtaining a consultant's recommendations, parents also should have extensive conversations with personnel from the program or school they are considering. If possible, parents should visit the program or school to see for themselves what it is like. When the parents and educational consultant disagree, it is important to remember that the parents have the final responsibility to decide what is best for their child.

Selecting a Program Primarily on the Basis of Cost

Programs and schools for struggling teens are expensive. They are costly to run. Some are sponsored by for-profit organizations that capitalize on parents' desperation to keep their struggling teens out of trouble with the law and safe from drug abuse, predators, sexually transmitted diseases, and pregnancy.

Parents may be tempted to save money by enrolling their child in the least expensive program or school available. In the long run, that may be a costly mistake; more expensive programs may not be better programs but a good fit between the program or school and the teen must be the primary goal. Choosing a less expensive placement that is not a good fit for the teen can lead to a "meltdown"; parents may then have a midyear crisis during which they must change the child's placement immediately, resulting in forfeiture of nonrefundable tuition and fees as well as having to move the child to perhaps an even more expensive placement. Finding the right program or school from the start can be the most cost-effective strategy in the long run. It also avoids disruption, upheaval, and heartache (see chapter 6 for discussion of options for financing specialty services and programs).

Selecting a Program That Is Not Designed to Meet the Teenager's Needs

Parents should get detailed information about the kinds of teenagers enrolled in the program or school the parents are considering. How closely do they resemble the teenager's mental health, behavioral, and educational challenges and needs? Is the program or school designed to meet the teenager's unique needs, or are the teenager's needs likely to be overlooked because they are different from those of the other teenagers in the program or school?

Selecting a Program Whose Methods Are Not Grounded in Sound Research

The most competent programs and schools base their approaches on what are known as "best practices." Best practices include treatment approaches, services, and educational models based on the latest theory and research published in reputable books and refereed or peer-reviewed professional journals (that is, professional journals that are more likely to have high academic standards). Do administrators monitor professional literature and research and use them to inform their program design and services? Staff in some programs may publish self-promoting manifestos that are little more than lengthy statements of belief and opinion and that are not grounded in a conceptual framework or research base. The attractive cover of the program or school catalog may be an effective marketing tool, but it does not necessarily reflect a reputable or high-quality program or school.

Sending a Child to a Residential Program for the Wrong Reasons

An out-of-home program or school may be necessary and the best option available, but a teenager should be sent to such a program for the right reasons. Parents should send their teen to a residential program or therapeutic boarding school because doing so is the best way to meet the child's needs. Sending the teen away primarily out of anger or frustration can be counterproductive and is likely to have damaging consequences. A teenager who feels "sent away" or "kicked out" of the family is likely to feel rejected, angry, unmotivated to address his or her issues, and hostile and may attempt to sabotage his or her own experience at the program or school by defying staff, breaking rules, or running away.

Avoiding Out-of-Home Placement When It Is the Right Option

Parents sometimes resist placing their teen in a residential treatment center or therapeutic boarding school because they cannot bear to "lose" their child, they do not trust strangers to give their child the care she or he needs, or they fear the child will feel rejected and expelled. Many struggling teens suffer from low self-esteem stemming from rejection by peers, school suspensions, foster placements, or adoption. Many parents are concerned that sending their child "away" for help will intensify that sense of rejection and compound the youth's problems.

Although those concerns may be well-founded for some teens, a residential program or boarding school may nonetheless be a good option. The program or school may remove the child from destructive peer relationships at home and provide the opportunity to interact with peers in a safe setting; provide the child with structure, some independence, and an opportunity to take stock of his or her life; and give "breathing room" that helps parents and children heal their relationship, communicate more effectively, and bond more closely. Ironically, geographical distance—with regular opportunities for contact by telephone, by e-mail, and during family weekends and vacations—often helps bring parents and their children closer together emotionally.

Selecting a Program because It Is Close to Home

Parents, understandably, want to keep their child nearby and do not want to send him or her away. It is hard to place one's struggling child in the hands of strangers. Keeping the child in a nearby program or school eases the pain of separation; however, the program or school that is close by may not be the one that can best meet the teenager's needs. Parents sometimes make the mistake of trading the most appropriate program or school for geographic proximity. Parents may need to take a deep breath and enroll their child in a program or school that requires a very long car, bus, or airplane trip.

Making Mistakes—and Learning from Them: One Family's Story

Eddie, 15, had done well in grade school. During those years, while he had few friends, he seemed content at school and got good grades. In middle school, however, things started to fall apart for Eddie. Peers picked on him relentlessly. The demands of middle school work overwhelmed Eddie. He had trouble keeping track of assignments, changing classrooms throughout the day, and completing homework. By the middle of the first term in seventh grade, Eddie was failing most subjects and was refusing to get out of bed in the morning to go to school. Eddie's parents started him in counseling with a clinical social worker; this therapist referred Eddie to a psychiatrist, who diagnosed Eddie with ADHD, posttraumatic stress disorder from the maltreatment by peers, and depression and started him on medication to brighten his mood, enhance focus and concentration, and reduce impulsivity. Eddie continued to struggle during the seventh- and eighth-grade years.

One day during Eddie's ninth-grade year, the school's vice principal called Eddie's parents to report that Eddie had been leaving school midday with several new friends; the kids were gathering in a nearby park to use drugs (marijuana, Ecstasy, OxyContin, and crystal methamphetamine). After receiving the telephone call, Eddie's father left work, went searching for him, and found him hanging out in the park; he had dilated pupils, bloodshot eyes, and slurred speech. When Eddie's father told him to come with him, Eddie screamed at him and tried to hit him. Eddie's dad put up his arms to ward off the blow, and Eddie yelled loudly, "Help me! He's beating me!" Eddie's dad was dumbfounded and horrified. He felt helpless, enraged, and frightened.

Eddie's parents immediately made an appointment with Eddie's clinical social worker, who began meeting with Eddie twice a week. The situation did not improve. Eddie lied to his therapist, was defiant at home, argued with his parents, ignored curfew, and refused to do school work. Often he would stay up all night, sneaking out of bed to trade instant messages with his friends on the computer. In the middle of one night, Eddie's mom heard strange noises and got up to investigate. She found Eddie leaning out his third-floor bedroom window throwing a sock stuffed with money to one of his new, drug-using friends. Eddie had stolen the money from his father's wallet.

In short, Eddie was out of control. Counseling was not working, and Eddie refused to abide by his parents' rules. His parents asked the school guidance counselor to have Eddie evaluated for an IEP so Eddie could get more supportive services at school. The school counselor agreed but said there was a six-month waiting list for evaluations. Eddie's parents feared for Eddie's safety during such a long wait.

Eddie's clinical social worker suggested that his parents enroll Eddie in a six-week wilderness therapy program based in Utah. The therapist had referred several other teenage clients to that program over the years and had gotten favorable feedback from them.

Eddie's parents refinanced their home to pay for the wilderness therapy program; fortunately, they received partial reimbursement from their health insurance company for the mental health services provided to Eddie during the program. Eddie did well in the program, was able to take some responsibility for his self-destructive choices in the past, and calmed down in the soothing desert environment free from the frantic electronic distractions surrounding teens in their home communities. At the end of the program, Eddie's primary wilderness program therapist explained to his parents that returning directly home would likely lead Eddie back into the waiting arms of his drug-using friends. The therapist said, "At least for now, Eddie should go to one of the boarding schools for struggling teens, a place with structure, supervision, and support to help him build on his progress in our program and stay on track. Given Eddie's need to fit in and his impulsivity, it may be hard for him to remain safe if he leaves here and heads right back to his old neighborhood."

Eddie's parents were alarmed. They had hoped that six weeks in the wilderness therapy program would set Eddie straight. They had no extra money for a follow-up program. Eddie's parents had missed him terribly while he had been away in the wilderness therapy program, and they did not want him to go away again. They knew nothing about specialty boarding schools and began gathering information. Because of the cost, they rejected the wilderness program therapist's advice about retaining an educational consultant to help them find a good boarding school; they decided to explore the options themselves. Their explorations quickly revealed that specialty boarding schools for struggling teens, like educational consultants, are very expensive. So Eddie's parents chose to bring him directly home from the wilderness therapy program and tried to structure and supervise his days as best they could. They kept Eddie in counseling, continued to pursue an IEP for him with local school officials, resumed family counseling to get new parenting ideas, and enrolled Eddie in an after-school program with structured activities for teens. They rearranged their work schedules so one parent would be home whenever Eddie was not at school.

Unfortunately, within two weeks Eddie's drug-using friends began to seek him out again. Eddie's parents watched their son struggle to resist the temptation to hang out with these peers. Clearly, Eddie had learned a lot during his wilderness therapy experience, but he was having a hard time avoiding his friends and familiar patterns.

Eddie's parents began to worry and decided to enroll him in a boarding school they had heard about that was only an hour's drive from their home and was much less expensive than the therapeutic boarding schools they had explored earlier.

The boarding school in which Eddie enrolled marketed itself as a school that provided "character" education. The admissions representative at the school, who was the parent of a former student at the school and did not have a formal academic degree in education or in a mental health field or in work with struggling teenagers, explained to the parents that the school is particularly skilled at confronting students' "poor attitudes" and building character.

Eddie wanted to stay out of trouble and solidify the progress he had made in the wilderness therapy program. He willingly entered the boarding school and looked forward to the new adventure, but within weeks at the new school, Eddie began having serious difficulty. He was often disciplined for having a "poor attitude" and "character flaws." Demoralized, frightened, and frustrated, Eddie developed suicidal ideation. The school did not assess Eddie's mental health status; in fact, the school did not employ any mental health professionals to address students' mental health needs, even though most students were "struggling teens" who had come to the school with a variety of mental health issues and learning disabilities. The school employed a general pediatric nurse to administer psychotropic medication, but only during hours convenient to the school, not at the times recommended by Eddie's psychiatrist. Despite his parents' pleas to the school to address Eddie's mental health issues, which seemed to explain the difficulties he was having, school administrators informed the parents that Eddie's symptoms were merely "excuses" and "manipulative ploys" and that Eddie's "attitude" and "character" were the problems. School personnel also accused Eddie's parents of being a major source of Eddie's troubles: "The apple doesn't fall far from the tree," staff told the parents.

Upon Eddie's enrollment, the boarding school had promised his parents a weekly telephone call from Eddie's adviser that would keep them abreast of Eddie's progress and coordinate care. Those telephone calls never came. When the parents called the school, they received short, perfunctory replies, such as, "We have a model that works. Let go. Trust us. If what you do at home worked, you wouldn't need us. Eddie has problems because of your attitude, which is what you should be focusing on." Eddie's parents decided to let the school do their "thing," believing that perhaps the school was right.

Eddie's parents' misgivings continued to grow, however. They learned that the school disciplined students, including Eddie, by requiring them to report for rigorous exercise at 5:30 a.m. As a result, those students were often sleep deprived, which exacerbated the difficulty they had complying with the school's rules. Also, in the school's mandatory family seminars, which Eddie's parents dutifully attended,

Eddie's parents watched seminar leaders routinely demand that participants disclose to strangers in the group intimate details about their lives. Seminar participants who showed any reluctance were confronted and shamed in front of the group. Occasionally, when children in the group broke down under the pressure, seminar leaders called them names, belittling and shaming them (for example, "You're a cry baby," "Shape up, grow up"). These seminars were facilitated by teachers at the school who had no formal education in how to handle the delicate and volatile mental health issues that emerged in the groups.

Eddie's parents reluctantly realized that the school's approach constituted emotional abuse. They told the school they wanted to withdraw Eddie. Unfortunately the school would not refund any of the parents' money. The parents consulted a lawyer who said the prospects of a refund were bleak because of the terms in the agreement they signed when they enrolled Eddie.

The parents finally realized they had made mistakes by bringing Eddie home directly from the wilderness therapy program, attempting to locate an appropriate boarding school without the help of a skilled educational consultant, and enrolling Eddie in a school that they selected because of its cost and proximity to their home. Having learned those lessons, Eddie's parents retained an educational consultant to help them locate a more appropriate boarding school. Within three weeks, Eddie transferred to a new boarding school that was particularly well-suited to his needs. His parents funded this new placement through educational loans and by liquidating a large portion of their retirement and college savings. Eddie's parents also began working part-time jobs to supplement their modest income from their full-time jobs.

The new school provided a much more nurturing environment, focused on students' strengths, collaborated conscientiously with parents, carefully considered and responded to students' mental health needs, placed students in much smaller classes, and held Eddie to high behavioral and academic standards. Within about six weeks of starting the new school, Eddie's mood brightened, he recommitted himself to school work, and he was compliant with the school's reasonable rules. Although Eddie struggled occasionally with his ADHD, posttraumatic stress disorder, and depression, over time his functioning improved dramatically. Eddie's parents were convinced that the constructive, supportive environment in the new school had made a tremendous difference. Although they no longer had money saved for Eddie's college education, they knew that Eddie would finish high school and be alive to go to college.

———————————

CHAPTER 3

A Guide to Services and Programs

Many different kinds of services and programs are available for struggling teens. Some provide relatively short-term crisis intervention, and others provide long-term care and treatment. Parents may find it useful to think about services and programs as a spectrum of options. At one end of the spectrum are services and programs that emphasize educational issues and, in addition, pay attention to teenagers' emotional needs. Examples include traditional high schools and alternative, community-based high schools that work with teens and parents to develop an IEP or 504 plan. At the other end of the spectrum are programs that focus primarily on struggling teens' psychiatric and emotional needs as well as provide teens with educational services. Examples include therapeutic boarding schools and residential treatment centers. In the middle of the spectrum are schools and programs that offer a balanced, simultaneous focus on teens' personal growth and educational needs (for example, "emotional-growth" boarding schools).

Generally, struggling teens should receive services in their home communities rather than in schools and programs away from home. Community-based services may increase the likelihood that a youth will stay in school and maintain important ties with supportive family members and friends. Of course, in some instances the best way to meet a struggling teen's needs is to enroll the teen in a specialty program or a school away from the home community. This approach may be necessary when the teen's unique needs cannot be met locally or when the teen would benefit from a completely new social environment, away from local distractions and negative influences.

Below is a comprehensive summary of services, programs, and schools for struggling teens. They are presented on a continuum, starting with home-based and community-based services and moving to residential programs and schools.[1]

Crisis Intervention

Many different professionals and agencies offer crisis intervention and follow-up counseling services to teens and families. The services may be available through family service agencies, community mental health centers, hospital outpatient clinics, public child welfare departments, and psychotherapists in private practice (for example, clinical social workers, clinical and counseling psychologists, mental health counselors, pastoral counselors, psychiatric nurses, psychiatrists).

Many communities offer comprehensive counseling and family-intervention programs specifically for teens and families in crisis. Those programs—known by names such as "comprehensive emergency services" or "comprehensive intensive services"—provide home-based assessment, emergency counseling, information, and referrals for long-term help. Some programs will arrange for experienced staff to visit families in their homes, observe family members' interactions, recommend interventions to enhance family functioning, and help the family implement the recommendations. Parents can locate services by consulting information and referral programs or by contacting local community mental health centers, family service agencies, hospital psychiatry and outpatient clinics, private counselors, clergy, and other organizations and professionals familiar with local mental health resources.

Crisis Intervention Steps

Parents of struggling teens face crises. Their child may be heading downhill fast as they stumble in school, hang out with the "wrong crowd," engage in high-risk behaviors, and defy their parents' authority. Crisis intervention professionals recommend seven steps to help youths in a crisis; these tips may be useful to parents of struggling teens who are trying to figure out the best course of action.

---

1. Program and school descriptions are included for illustrative purposes only. The descriptions do not constitute endorsements. They provide a range of examples drawn from various geographical regions.

1. *Stabilize the situation.* Determine the severity of the crisis and try to prevent immediate harm to the teenager and other people. At this stage, it is vitally important to use good listening skills, establish a trusting and sincere relationship, and help the teenager identify and cope with his or her feelings (for example, anger, frustration, and despair). Focusing on the teenager's strengths and past successes dealing with crises can be helpful.
2. *Assess the risk.* Determine whether the teenager is suicidal or has plans to harm other people.
3. *Identify the major problems.* Explore the teenager's concerns and try to identify what precipitated the crisis. What circumstances surrounded and led up to the crisis (for example, breaking up with a girlfriend or boyfriend, drug overdose, pregnancy, arrest by the police, fight with parents)? How do the teenager and other important people in his or her life understand what happened and why it happened?
4. *Identify responsible adults.* Who are the adults in the teenager's life who need to know about the crisis? With whom does the teenager have a good relationship? Which adults can provide support during the crisis (for example, parents, neighbors, relatives, a favorite teacher, counselor, clergy)?
5. *Identify and explore alternatives and determine what services are needed.* Identify resources that the teenager has used successfully in the past, including school counselors, therapists, family friends, parents, teachers, clergy, or social service agencies. Would crisis counseling be useful? Is psychiatric hospitalization or referral to a drug or alcohol treatment program necessary? It may be useful to identify short-term and long-term goals.
6. *Arrange for services.* Contact professionals and other responsible adults who can assist with referrals and the provision of services. Crisis centers, community mental health centers, family service agencies, and inpatient and outpatient mental health programs may be able to provide help arranging services.
7. *Follow up.* Be sure to follow up to see that the teenager and responsible adults in his or her life have made contact with appropriate professionals and that an appropriate plan for services is in place.

Specialty Courts

Many communities have developed specialty courts to intervene early when youths begin to show signs that they are struggling. Specialty courts typically focus on substance abuse and truancy issues.

Substance Abuse Courts

Many communities sponsor substance abuse courts, also known as drug courts. These specialty courts use a supportive and nurturing approach rather than a punitive one to help struggling teens. Using case management, counseling, tutoring, mentoring, and parent education, the goal of the substance abuse court is to help the teen to prevent future problems and more formal involvement with the juvenile justice system.

Substance abuse courts integrate alcohol and other drug treatment services with justice system case processing. Using a nonadversarial approach, prosecution and defense counsel attempt to address teenagers' substance abuse issues and promote public safety while protecting participants' due process rights. Typically, eligible participants are identified early in the judicial process—usually soon after arrest—and promptly placed in the substance abuse court program. Substance abuse courts provide access to a continuum of alcohol, drug, and related treatment. Teenagers enrolled in the program are monitored by frequent alcohol and other drug testing.

A Substance Abuse Court: The Santa Barbara (California) Substance Abuse Treatment Court

The Santa Barbara (California) Substance Abuse Treatment Court combines the close supervision of the judicial process with alcohol and drug treatment services. The court's goal is to reduce recidivism by maintaining drug offenders in a highly structured treatment setting until they show evidence of clean and sober lifestyles. The program allows serious drug offenders to participate in 18 months of supervised treatment under a single treatment provider to earn a dismissal of the criminal charge. A second program provides an opportunity for offenders on probation to participate in 12 months of supervised treatment offered by several community-based treatment providers as an alternative to a jail or prison sentence. These programs are for nonviolent offenders who demonstrate evidence of alcohol or drug abuse. The participants are identified early in the court process by probation officers, prosecutors, defense attorneys, and judges. Defendants charged with drug possession; drug use; or other nonviolent offenses, such as theft, are considered for drug court programs if evidence indicates that serious substance abuse is a primary cause of the criminal behavior.

Under the program, the offender pleads guilty and participates in court-monitored treatment as a condition of probation. The offender agrees that failure to participate in the treatment program satisfactorily will result in a trial in which the judge only has to read the police report to determine whether the defendant is guilty. For each offender, a treatment plan is developed that includes individual and group counseling, frequent drug testing, acupuncture to reduce cravings, regular Alcoholics Anonymous or Narcotics Anonymous meetings, and weekly court appearances. To graduate, the offender must complete the entire course of treatment and must have had no "dirty" drug tests or program violations for at least six months. Any failure in program participation or dirty drug tests is dealt with by use of graduated sanctions ranging from increased program participation to incarceration.

Truancy Courts

Many communities sponsor truancy courts for teenagers who have skipped significant numbers of school days. Research shows that truancy is often a correlate and predictor of other substantial problems in teenagers' lives. As do substance abuse courts, truancy courts use a supportive and nurturing approach rather than a punitive one to help struggling teens. Using case management, counseling, tutoring, mentoring, and parent education, the truancy court's goal is to help the teen to prevent future problems and more formal involvement with the juvenile justice system.

Truancy courts, like substance abuse courts, integrate counseling and other social services with justice system case processing. Using a nonadversarial approach, prosecution and defense counsel attempt to simultaneously address teenagers' truancy issues and promote public safety while protecting participants' due process rights. Truancy courts provide access to a continuum of mental health, case management, educational, and substance abuse services. Teenagers enrolled in the program are monitored frequently.

A Truancy Court: Students Achieving School Success

The Students Achieving School Success program in Madison County, Kentucky, is designed to assist students and families in identifying problems associated with school attendance and then work as a team to find methods for solving the problems. The truancy court program arranges informal hearings that occur in a school setting prior to the filing of formal charges to divert truancy or educational neglect cases from district and family courts.

The Madison County program is a collaborative effort involving the local Board of Education, Family Court, and Youth Service Center (YSC). Students who have more than nine unexcused absences are referred to the program. Staff of the YSC meet with students and parents and inform them that if they successfully complete the program they can avoid having formal charges filed with the courts. Students and their parents are required to attend eight sessions that are held at the school every two weeks.

During the truancy court sessions, the judge focuses not only on the student's attendance record but also on academic performance and school behavior. Teachers of a student in the program complete a form every two weeks that provides the court with feedback on the youth's progress. If the student's performance does not improve, the student may be required to attend an after-school program for a specified period of time.

At the end of the semester, students whose attendance has improved graduate from the program. Those who continue to have unexcused absences will repeat the program during the following semester or a petition will be filed, leading to formal processing of the youth's case in court.

The program includes an aftercare phase in which staff monitor the youth's attendance for one semester following exit from the program. In addition, parents and students are required to attend the first truancy court session of the semester following completion of the program so that the judge and staff can reinforce the importance of continuing to attend school regularly.

_____

Specialty Schools and Programs

A variety of alternative schools, therapeutic schools, and treatment programs serve teens who struggle with significant behavioral, emotional, mental health, substance abuse, and educational issues. Some programs, such as alternative high schools, focus primarily on education while being sensitive to students' mental health and behavioral challenges. Other programs, such as residential treatment programs, therapeutic boarding schools, and wilderness therapy programs, focus primarily on mental health, emotional, and behavioral issues while including an educational component. Emotional-growth boarding schools address mental health, emotional, behavioral, and educational issues simultaneously. Other boarding schools focus on learning disabilities while paying attention to the whole student. In short, different programs and schools give different degrees of emphasis to personal and academic issues.

Parents of a struggling teen—particularly a teen who is not fulfilling academic potential or who is oppositional and defiant—naturally want to place their child in a school or program that promises to impose needed discipline and structure. Some of these schools and programs—such as some military boarding schools and those that advertise their mission as "character education"—do not provide the mental health services many struggling teens need. They can cause more harm than good for struggling teens who have personal, emotional, or mental health issues that contribute to their challenges.

Alternative High Schools

Alternative high schools in the home community provide education, including special education services, to teens who have foundered academically or socially in traditional high schools. The schools may be freestanding or sponsored by a community mental health center, family services agency, school district, or "collaborative" composed of several social services and educational programs.

Alternative schools tend to serve students who respond well to a smaller and a more individualized academic program than is typically available in traditional high schools. Alternative schools may provide frequent opportunities for students to express themselves creatively through music, art, drama, and writing. Many alternative schools encourage students to do community-based internships in local organizations, agencies, and businesses. They also emphasize student-led initiatives and encourage relationships between students and mentors or coaches. Creative, nontraditional approaches also are used during class sessions to engage students who have foundered in other school settings, for example, encouraging students to use video equipment or dramatic presentations to communicate their ideas.

Alternative high schools tend not to arrange classrooms in rows of desks, favoring instead seats around tables that facilitate discussion. In many alternative high schools, rather than assign students traditional grades, teachers write detailed narrative assessments that summarize students' progress, successes, challenges, and learning needs.

An Alternative High School: School One

School One is an alternative high school in Providence, Rhode Island. School One provides its culturally diverse student body with small classes (five to 15 students), personalized advisement, and a strong emphasis on the arts. The school serves no more than 100 students. A personal educational plan is developed for each student according to his or her unique goals, interests, strengths, and challenges. Students receive a comprehensive assessment of their progress rather than traditional grades along with pass–fail assessments of their classroom work and extracurricular activities.

Each student selects an adviser from among the school's faculty. The advisers coach, counsel, and mentor their students. Advisers also help students with postgraduate planning. School One actively integrates the arts into its curriculum. Courses that include painting, drawing, photography, ceramics, video, and performing arts encourage students' exploration, creativity, and constructive experimentation.

School One is a member of the Coalition of Essential Schools (CES), a national group of schools that seeks to reform education in the United States. Currently the CES network includes approximately

600 schools. These schools base their teaching and curriculum on a series of core common principles—grounded in theory and extensive research—that are particularly well suited for struggling teens who are more likely to thrive in nontraditional school settings, including personalized instruction to address individual needs and interests; small schools and classrooms, where teachers and students know each other well and work in an atmosphere of trust and high expectations; multiple assessments that are based on performance of authentic tasks; democratic and equitable school policies and practices; and close partnerships with the school community.

Youth Diversion Programs

Youth diversion programs typically attempt to help struggling teens who have had contact with the police avoid more formal involvement in the juvenile justice system (that is, juvenile courts and correctional facilities). Typical youth diversion programs offer first-time offenders individual and family counseling, links to other needed services (such as psychiatric medication), and education. Juveniles enrolled in diversion programs typically meet with probation officers who provide the court with periodic progress reports. Teens who comply with youth diversion program requirements may be able to avoid formal court adjudication and intervention.

"Outreach and tracking" is one type of diversion program used in many communities. The staff of these programs initiate face-to-face contact with the struggling teen several times a day, seven days a week, to provide close monitoring. The goal is to keep the teenager safe in the community, in the family, in school, and out of trouble.

A Youth Diversion Program: The Tempe (Arizona) Youth Diversion Program

The Tempe Youth Diversion Program operates with the cooperation of the Maricopa County (Arizona) Juvenile Court Probation Department and the Tempe Municipal Court. The program diverts first-time offenders from the juvenile justice system. Teenagers who participate in diversion avoid formal contact with the juvenile court and instead are involved in a structured, community-based program. Eligible offenses include shoplifting, petty theft, trespassing, destruction of property, curfew violation, alcohol violation, and running away from home.

The Maricopa County Juvenile Court or Tempe Municipal Court refers the teenager and his or her parents for an intake interview with one of the program's counselors, who conducts an assessment to develop an individualized program that addresses the teenager's unique needs. The diversion plan may require individual, family, or group counseling; educational workshops on topics such as substance abuse issues or domestic violence; volunteer work at a nonprofit agency in the community; restitution; or participation in an employment program. The primary goals of the diversion program are to encourage at-risk teenagers to engage in more positive and constructive behavior; intervene with the teen at an early stage and avoid the possibility of progression toward more serious offenses; help the teen avoid the negative connotations associated with formal referral to juvenile court; and provide the teenager and family with appropriate social services.

Mentoring Programs

Mentoring programs provide struggling teens with trained, caring adults who provide teens with support, guidance, advice, and friendship. Mentoring programs encourage teens to stay focused on their education; provide support during crises; offer constructive ways to spend free time; and expose teens to career paths and options. Mentors seek to enhance, but not replace, the roles of parents, guardians, and teachers. Mentors and teens may begin their relationship by participating in a variety of activities. Depending on the type of mentoring program—and the program's rules and regulations—a mentoring pair may begin getting to know each other by going to a local gym, playground, museum, restaurant, athletic event, or rock concert. Mentors and mentees might also meet at the child's school once a week, where they might talk or work on schoolwork together.

A Teen Mentoring Program: YES Mentoring

The YES (Youth Empowerment for Success) Mentoring Program is sponsored by the Children's Aid Society in New York City. The program focuses on black and Latino youths. The program matches teens with adult volunteers of similar gender, ethnicity, and cultural background. Through weekly groups, monthly activities, and the mentoring relationship, adolescent boys and girls develop a sense of culture and identity along with responsibility for their community. YES is a Brooklyn Persons in Need of Supervision (PINS) program; its goal is to provide meaningful ongoing relationships that expose youths to significant educational, social, and cultural opportunities; increase self-esteem; and foster positive behavioral changes. Mentors may choose to participate in monthly group activities as part of their time requirements or may choose to meet separately with their mentee. Mentors are included in group programming, family sessions and, often, on home visits conducted by caseworkers and social workers. Volunteers commit at least four hours per month to work with teens.

Day Treatment Programs

Day treatment programs provide teens with nonresidential services to help them address their mental health and substance abuse issues. Typical programs require youths to participate in individual, group, and, when feasible, family counseling. Educational services may be included to help teens stay on track academically.

A Day Treatment Program: Rogers Memorial Hospital

The Day Treatment Program at Rogers Memorial Hospital in Milwaukee, Wisconsin, offers half-day structured treatment for adolescents. This program provides intensive treatment while allowing continued involvement in everyday activities with family and school. The day treatment program addresses issues such as severe mood swings; school problems; defiance issues; frequent rage, outbursts, or threats; isolation or withdrawal; alcohol and drug problems; ADHD; depression; and anxiety. Adolescents meet individually with staff members to develop an individualized treatment plan. Treatment may consist of several types of therapy, such as individual counseling; group therapy;

family therapy; experiential and expressive therapies, such as recreation, art, music, and drama therapy; cognitive–behavioral therapy; and medication management. Half-day sessions are held Monday through Friday from 8:00 a.m. to 11:30 a.m. or 12:30 p.m. to 4:00 p.m. The treatment team includes practitioners from the fields of psychiatry, social work, psychology, family therapy, nursing, and education.

Partial Hospitalization Programs

Partial hospitalization programs are for teens with serious mental health issues. The programs are an alternative to residential treatment or inpatient hospitalization. Partial hospitalization programs are designed to fill most of the teen's daily waking hours Monday through Friday and provide a therapeutic milieu that includes psychiatric medication management; individual, family, and group therapy; psychoeducation; and occupational and recreational therapy. Usually, teens attending a partial hospitalization program sleep at home in the evenings or live in a group home or foster home, and they travel to the partial hospitalization program on weekdays.

A Partial Hospitalization Program: Kahi Mohala Behavioral Health

The Adolescent Partial Hospitalization Program at Kahi Mohala Behavioral Health, in Ewa Beach, Hawaii, is designed for adolescents ages 13 to 18 who are unable to function because of emotional or behavioral difficulties.

Teens in this program exhibit psychiatric symptoms or behavior problems that impair their day-to-day educational, social, vocational, or interpersonal functioning; have had difficulty progressing in other outpatient settings; do not pose an imminent threat to themselves or others; and have access to community supports while enrolled in the program. Some teens are admitted when they are ready for discharge from an inpatient or residential setting and would benefit from the transition that partial hospitalization provides.

The Adolescent Partial Hospitalization Program is located in a separate building on the grounds of Kahi Mohala Behavioral Health, a psychiatric hospital. A common area, a group room, and a resource/multipurpose room are in the building to facilitate a self-contained program that also has access to hospital facilities such as the dining room, specialized therapy clinics, gymnasium, and a Reality-Oriented Physical Experiential Services therapeutic challenge course. Program hours are Monday through Friday, 9 a.m. to 3 p.m., and the program operates year-round. Services include counseling, health education, occupational and recreational therapy, and medication evaluation and management. Family therapy is arranged as needed.

Group Homes

Group homes provide teens with structured, supervised out-of-home care. Teens are placed in a group home when living with their family is not realistic or appropriate. Group homes typically provide shelter and a wide range of mental health, educational, and recreational services. Lengths of stay vary considerably depending on the teen's unique needs and family circumstances.

Adolescent Group Home:
Shelter, Inc.

The adolescent group home operated by Shelter, Inc., in Arlington Heights, Illinois, serves older adolescents who have been abused or neglected or are struggling. Many of the program's participants have struggled with mental health, substance abuse, and educational issues. Most come to the program from unstable families. Youths may stay in the program for up to two years.

In addition to housing, the program provides youths with individual and group counseling, health care, educational services, independent living skills, and follow-up services. The program staff teach residents how to develop interpersonal relationship skills; plan, shop, and prepare meals; find and keep a job; and manage money.

Wilderness Therapy Programs

Wilderness therapy programs, also known as outdoor behavioral health programs, offer highly structured, intensive short-term (usually three to eight weeks) therapy in remote locations that remove adolescents from the distractions of their home communities (for example, television, music, computers, cars, drugs and alcohol, movies, delinquent peer groups). The natural challenges of living outdoors full-time and developing wilderness survival skills help teens develop self-confidence, take responsibility for their choices, experience the natural consequences of their behaviors, and develop problem-solving and social skills under the guidance of therapeutic staff.

Typical wilderness therapy programs provide counseling, education, leadership training, and survival-skill challenges that strengthen a teenager's ability to function in a community of people. Programs foster interdependence and seek to enhance teenagers' honesty, awareness, openness, accountability, and responsibility. Common wilderness therapy activities include outdoor education, primitive living, team-building exercises, structured daily activities, individual and group counseling, and expeditions.

A key goal of wilderness therapy programs is to give teenagers opportunities to experience the natural consequences of their decisions and actions. For example, if a defiant teen refuses to learn how to build a campfire without matches, he or she will be cold as the sun sets and unable to prepare and eat dinner. If an oppositional teen refuses to put plastic under his or her sleeping bag, the teen will be uncomfortably wet if it rains heavily during the night. These experiences help defiant teens learn what they can and cannot control in life. That is, one cannot control the rain but one can control how one copes with the rain. Ideally, teens transfer this understanding to their lives back home.

Often, families are advised to send their struggling teen first to a wilderness therapy program and then to a therapeutic or emotional-growth boarding school, rather than return the teen to his or her home community environment directly from the wilderness. Ideally, the wilderness therapy program "jump starts" the teen's readiness for self-exploration and the personal growth process by taking the youth out of his or her "comfort zone" and the familiar home environment where she or he managed to manipulate or control authority figures. Returning directly from the wilderness therapy program to the barrage of negative peer influences in the home community can quickly undo the benefits gained from the wilderness therapy experience. The wilderness therapy program primes the pump to enhance the effectiveness of the emotional growth or therapeutic boarding school.[2]

A Wilderness Therapy Program: Second Nature

Second Nature is a wilderness therapy program that operates in remote locations in Utah, Oregon, and Georgia. Typical teenagers enrolled in Second Nature are coping with a variety of emotional, behavioral, and educational struggles such as depression, substance abuse, oppositional defiant disorder, and learning disabilities that negatively affect school performance and interpersonal relationships. Students may isolate themselves, expect instant gratification, or act entitled. They may be self-medicating, battling their parents, and failing to respond to limits and rules.

As with most wilderness therapy programs, Second Nature steers a student's progress through several phases. Upon arrival, the student receives a physical examination, clothing, and gear (for example, backpack, sleeping bag and pad, shelter tarp, jackets, pants and shorts, hiking boots, camp shoes). Then the student is transported to the small group with which the student will be living in the wilderness during the program stay. During the first 24 to 48 hours, the student is physically separated from the group; the student may sit under a nearby tree and watch the group but is not allowed to enter the group. This gives the teen a safe space in which to withdraw from any illegal drugs, allows staff to observe the teen's coping style, and helps the student feel prepared to join the group rather than isolate and withdraw. During this time, the student is asked to complete individual assignments, observe group dynamics, and decide to comply with the program.

---

2. Some defiant teens refuse to go voluntarily to a wilderness therapy program, therapeutic boarding school, or residential treatment program. In those cases, parents may need to hire specially trained professionals who transport the teen to the destination. Teen transport professionals are trained in nonviolent crisis intervention techniques, crisis de-escalation, anger management, suicide awareness and prevention, and conflict resolution. They accompany the teen on the trip to the program or school to ensure safety and compliance during the travel.

This introductory phase gives students space to feel emotions (anger, fear, sadness); adjust to their loss of freedom and contact with family, friends, and modern conveniences; and accept the reality of the new peer group and wilderness environment. During this stage, students are asked to write their life stories, write letters to parents acknowledging the impact of their behaviors on the family and others, and learn about low-impact camping and backcountry skills (for example, tying knots, building fires and shelters, nutrition, hygiene).

During the second phase, Second Nature students focus on how past and current behaviors affect their short- and long-term options. Students learn about the importance of relationships with others, basic communication skills, and the value of personal responsibility. Assignments during this stage are designed to motivate the students to accept responsibility for their actions, express themselves both verbally and in writing, and begin the differentiation process from friends and family.

During the third phase, students are expected to assume more and more leadership responsibility with other students. For many students, this is the first opportunity to mentor, lead, and guide others. Students may lead a group hike through the forest and mentor a new student while they continue to work on their personal and family issues.

In the next-to-last phase, students who have made considerable progress are assigned more and more responsibility for the group and given additional privileges. They may be asked to join staff in planning activities, develop their own therapy assignments, and help the group resolve issues.

The final "transition" phase focuses on the next steps in the student's life. During this period, students receive more freedom and privileges as they demonstrate leadership, personal responsibility, appropriate interactions with others, problem-solving skills, effective communication skills, awareness of strengths, and reconnection with family. Staff work with students and parents to develop appropriate aftercare plans, which may include transitioning to a residential treatment program or therapeutic boarding school.

Boarding Schools for Teens with Learning Disabilities

Boarding schools for teens with learning disabilities offer structured academic programs that focus on teens' learning differences while addressing relevant emotional and behavioral issues. Boarding schools for this population provide special education and counseling services to help students with their academic, emotional, and behavioral challenges. Students with learning differences may face any number of educational challenges. Often social skills issues accompany learning disabilities. After years of school struggles, teens who have learning differences also may have developed depression and anxiety and feel profoundly disheartened, inferior, inadequate, ashamed, and excluded. Hence, a boarding school can provide a positive social opportunity as well as academic supports that enable the youth to succeed academically.

A Boarding School for Teenagers with Learning Disabilities: Eagle Hill School

The Eagle Hill School in Hardwick, Massachusetts, serves teenagers with a range of learning disabilities, including ADHD. The school provides students with special education services tailored to each student's learning differences and special needs. Students live in small dormitory settings with live-in resident counselors. In addition to the academic program, students are offered a rich variety of social, recreational, cultural, and athletic activities that are sensitive to the range of students' strengths and challenges.

Emotional-Growth Boarding Schools

Emotional-growth boarding schools offer structured academic programs and focus on emotional development and personal growth, but they do not provide the intensive treatment services offered by therapeutic boarding schools. These schools cater especially to nontraditional students struggling with motivational and self-esteem issues. Typical students have a history of academic and personal underperformance; in traditional school settings, they may have acted out and posed behavioral challenges. Many students who enroll in emotional-growth boarding schools resemble students who attend alternative high schools.

Emotional-growth schools are similar to traditional boarding schools in some respects: They have structured and supervised daily schedules, afternoon and weekend activities, cultural events, and athletics. In addition, they tend to provide a nurturing, supportive setting that offers personal counseling within the academic environment. Some emotional-growth boarding schools offer group and individual therapy; others arrange for students to receive counseling from a therapist in the local community. Emotional-growth boarding schools actively provide students with emotional support and guidance; students receive frequent messages that their contributions are valued and that they are important members of the community. Academic and residential-life staff may use experiential learning exercises to help students develop a more positive sense of self and improve decision-making, problem-solving, and interpersonal skills.

An Emotional-Growth Boarding School: Rock Point School

The Rock Point School in Burlington, Vermont, is a small, co-ed emotional-growth boarding school serving 40 students in grades 9 through 12. The school offers small class size for individualized attention; the teacher–student ratio is approximately 1 to 10 in English, history, science, and art classes and 1 to 4 in math. Rock Point describes its students as creative, self-aware young people who have found themselves off track personally or academically and are ready to make positive changes to build fulfilling, healthy lives. Many students choose Rock Point after becoming disillusioned with large, impersonal high schools. Some come to strengthen their skills for living harmoniously with others. According to school administrators, "the entire Rock Point community is like a large family, with all the accompanying love and frustrations. Faculty and staff challenge students to understand and embody responsibility, honesty, generosity, and respect for others." Teachers and dorm staff meet with students in one-on-one and small-group settings to work on social, coping, and problem-solving skills. Staff work "with each student at a pace that is consistently challenging and supportive." The school uses a "level system"—that is, each student enjoys privileges tailored to her or his behavior both in and out of the classroom.

Therapeutic Boarding Schools

Therapeutic boarding schools focus intensively on students' mental health, substance abuse, and behavioral needs while providing an academic educational program. Therapeutic boarding schools place much more explicit daily emphasis on mental health counseling and treatment than do emotional-growth boarding schools. A typical therapeutic boarding school will devote significant amounts of structured time to individual counseling, group counseling, and substance abuse counseling. Students admitted to therapeutic boarding schools typically have a mental health diagnosis and are often described as impulsive, underachieving, defiant, and oppositional; they may have struggled with substance abuse and sexual acting out. Many therapeutic boarding schools require that the student first complete a wilderness therapy program before enrolling.

A Therapeutic Boarding School: Academy at Swift River

The Academy at Swift River in Cummington, Massachusetts, is a therapeutic boarding school that offers a highly structured 15-month program for students who have struggled in traditional settings and have histories of impulsive, underachieving, defiant, and oppositional behavior. Many students have struggled with substance abuse. During their stay students follow a highly structured daily schedule of classes, study halls, and physical exercise. Students complete a four-part series of academic, personal growth, social, and family seminars that parents attend. Individual and group counseling are included in the program. Students have no access to television, radio, or the Internet. They may call their parents weekly. Toward the end of their stay, students participate in three to five weeks of activities designed to teach volunteerism and community service to vulnerable populations. Many students enroll in college following completion of the program.

Residential Treatment Centers

Residential treatment centers offer highly structured treatment addressing substance abuse, family, and other mental health issues. In contrast with therapeutic boarding schools, residential treatment centers are more like a psychiatric facility than a school, although they may have an academic component in their programs. Teenagers admitted to residential treatment centers often manifest behaviors such as difficulty managing anger, frequent changes in behavior and mood, difficulty getting along with others, drug and alcohol abuse, defiance, manipulation, poor school performance, intentionally frightening and threatening others, threatening suicide, and destroying property. Teenagers admitted to a residential treatment center require intensive 24-hour supervision, intensive individual and group therapy, highly structured activities, and a positive peer environment. Residential treatment centers may also offer ambitious academic programs, including college prep curricula.

Some teenagers enter residential treatment centers after brief psychiatric hospitalization. Lengths of stay vary considerably, depending on the nature of the teenager's clinical and behavioral history and needs and the availability of appropriate follow-up services and programs, such as therapeutic boarding schools and emotional-growth boarding schools.

A Residential Treatment Center: Island View

The Island View residential treatment center in Syracuse, Utah, offers struggling teens long-term mental health services. Teens admitted to Island View typically have been defiant, performed poorly in traditional academic settings, struggled with mental health issues, abused drugs and alcohol, and have had difficulty getting along with others. Island View offers teenagers intensive individual, group, and family therapy; a positive peer environment; education; and activity and recreational services. Each youth receives an individualized treatment plan that focuses on communication and relationship skills, prosocial attitudes and behaviors, and personal insight. Students receive individual psychotherapy at least once a week and participate in group therapy two to three times a week. Parents join the students for weekly family therapy sessions via conference telephone calls. Parents also participate in quarterly parent seminars held on the campus and attend regional parent seminars held in different areas throughout the United States. Students may participate in a variety of weekly specialty groups devoted to topics such as chemical abuse and dependency; grief and loss; art therapy; adoption; emotional regulation; men's issues; women's issues; and social skills.

CHAPTER 4

Coping Guide for Parents:

How Do We Get Through This?

Many struggling teens have long histories of challenge. They may have been born with irritable and inflexible temperaments, mental health issues, and learning disabilities. By the time they have reached adolescence, they and their families may feel weary of the struggle as well as frustrated, angry, despairing, and fearful. Yet, parents hang on to the hope that love, nurture, and discipline will lead to positive outcomes. Virtually all parents of struggling teens have done their best to raise their children skillfully. By the time parents are ready to explore a program or school specifically designed for struggling teens, most have sought help from family, friends, teachers and other school staff, clergy, and outpatient therapists. Although some parents search for a program or school under relatively calm circumstances, many feel an intense sense of urgency and panic.

Veteran parents of struggling teens have learned a lot about how to cope. The following ideas may be helpful.

Provide Structure and Supervision
to Struggling Teens

Many struggling teens rebel against structure. They thrive on challenging rules set by parents, schools, police, employers, and others in positions of authority. Teenagers who abuse drugs, ignore curfews, act belligerently toward important people in their lives, and otherwise defy authority seem to be screaming with every breath that they want to be on their own and left alone to do as they please. Yet, ironically, these teenagers crave structure and predictability in their lives, although they may not know or admit it.

Some struggling teens challenge authority because of their deep-seated hurt and resentment toward others who, they believe, have hurt them. In fact, some of these teens have been deeply harmed and victimized by important adults in their lives (perhaps a noncustodial parent; an adult who sexually abused them; a birth parent who freed them for adoption; or a parent whose own health, mental health, or substance abuse issues have preoccupied them). Other teens act out because they have had too few limits set for them. Still other teenagers with stable families and conscientious parents act out because their inborn biochemistry and brain circuitry made them vulnerable to mood, anxiety, impulse-control problems, and information-processing disorders that cause misbehavior.

Whatever the circumstances that precede teenagers' struggles, both research evidence and professional wisdom show that consistent structure is essential. It is important, however, to distinguish between constructive structure and rigid rules. Parents who impose structure by "laying down the law" may, paradoxically, be counterproductive and stimulate rebellious behavior. Although some teenagers may respond to an iron-fist approach, many will not. Teenagers generally respond more cooperatively to consistent rules and limits presented in a gentle, fair, respectful way and, when appropriate, negotiated through communication and reasonable compromise. This is a tenuous tightrope for parents to walk—being firm, clear, and consistent with nonnegotiable rules while being responsive to the teenager's (sometimes provocative) voice. The balance required on this tightrope varies from child to child.

Take a close look at the most effective residential treatment centers, therapeutic boarding schools, emotional-growth boarding schools, and wilderness therapy programs. What they have in common is structure. Effective programs establish firm and fair ground rules regarding teenagers' conduct and impose reasonable sanctions when teens violate those rules. In residential programs and boarding schools, teens understand what constitutes appropriate behavior, language, and decorum. They know they are not allowed to fight, swear, insult others, use drugs, or engage in sexual activity or harassment. They understand the concept of gradual and intermediate sanctions, where modest misbehavior is met with modest sanctions (for example, missing out on an appealing social activity, losing phone privileges, or having to spend study hall time in a common area rather than in the privacy of one's room) and serious misbehavior is met with serious sanctions (for example, suspension or expulsion).

These same principles can be applied to parenting. Struggling teens do not do well with laissez-faire parenting. They need, and often respond to, close and respectful monitoring and supervision. Punitive, controlling, shaming consequences may squelch misbehavior in the short run but ultimately may fundamentally damage the parent–child relationship and stimulate rage-filled outbursts. Parents of struggling teens may find it helpful to keep the following guidelines in mind as they strive to introduce appropriate structure and supervision:[1]

▲ Remember, virtually every child wants to have a good relationship with his or her parents, to succeed in life, to have friends, and to do well in school. Inborn challenges and difficult life circumstances may put these successes out of a teen's easy reach. The struggling teen needs understanding and compassion as well as structure and discipline. Telling the teen who has ADHD to "just focus" is akin to telling a blind person "just open your eyes and see!" The person without eyes can learn to "see" with her or his fingers, ears, nose, and tongue. Similarly, the person with ADHD can learn to focus with individualized coping strategies and medication. In both cases, tailored supports are essential.

▲ Educate yourself about adolescent development. Learn about the behaviors to expect, the effects of physical changes, and ways to help your teenager deal with change. Knowing what challenges typical teens face can help parents weather storms and hang on to hope. Adolescents do grow out of some struggles.

▲ Remember your own adolescence, your changing feelings, anger at authority, and fears and hopes. Look at your adolescent's behavior in the context of those memories to help keep perspective. Remember,

---

1. Portions of these guidelines are adapted from recommendations developed by the National Clearinghouse on Families & Youth under the auspices of the Administration for Children and Families, Administration on Children, Youth and Families, Family and Youth Services Bureau, U.S. Department of Health and Human Services (available at http://www.ncfy.com/supporti.htm).

though, that each person is different; your child may experience adolescence differently from the way you did.

▲ Join a parents support group or take a course on how to parent teens. Parenting is a learned skill. Peer support and education can help even experienced parents by giving them new ideas and coping strategies.

▲ Listen more than talk. Whether they show it or not, teens have heard what their parents have told them all their lives. The more parents repeat the same lectures, warnings, and threats, the less the teen pays attention. Keep lectures short (for example, "When you leave the kitchen a mess, I feel upset. I want you to clean the kitchen after you've used it. When you do that, we'll argue less and have a better relationship.").

▲ Show your adolescent how to delight in life's pleasures and how to cope with the hard times. The beliefs that life should be fair and that one should always be happy can lead to frustration. Today's teens tend to feel that having fun is a "right" they are due. The peer culture promulgates this myth. Parents' voices can get lost in the cacophony.

▲ Reward good behavior by telling your teen how good it feels to you when you see him or her follow the rules. Positive reinforcement is far more effective than criticism or punishment. Words that belittle irreparably harm your relationship with your child.

▲ Teach your adolescent that rights and responsibilities go hand in hand, and give your child increasing responsibility for his or her personal well-being and that of the family. Many teens respond well when they have opportunities to show they are able to responsibly handle gradually increasing freedom and independence. When an adolescent's behavior is out of control, a parent naturally and rightfully tends to assert limits to keep their child out of harm's way. Once the teen's behavior is more compliant, it is important to let the leash out gradually so the teen learns that responsible behavior leads to more freedom. Understandably, parents may be hesitant to allow more freedom, for fear that their child will free-fall back to the days of defiance. At some point, however, holding the teen back can in and of itself lead to meltdown.

▲ Spend quality **and** quantity time with your adolescent. Adolescents naturally pull away from the family and spend more time at school, with friends, or at a job. Still, some time spent with caring parents is key to a teenager's ability to grow emotionally and socially. Take advantage of times when your teen is home, over dinner or watching television, to continue building your relationship. Know about your child's outside interests. The trick is to be present and attentive without hovering and being intrusive.

▲ Encourage other caring adults, including friends and relatives, to spend time with your teenager. Aunts and uncles or adult neighbors can offer your teen additional support, guidance, and attention.

▲ Accept that you have feelings, too. You may feel frustrated, angry, discouraged, or sad during difficult times with your teen. Being a good parent does not mean being perfect. Model the ability to apologize when you have let your emotions get the best of you. Your apology will help your child understand human frailty and will model how to mend a strained relationship. Rupture happens in all parent–child relationships. Repair is what matters.

▲ Many parents of struggling teens ask themselves, "Where did I go wrong? What did I do to make my child be like this? What should I have done differently?" Parents who have been preoccupied with their own struggles (for example, substance abuse, infidelity, contentious divorce, explosive temper, obsession with work) may feel guilty about how their issues have hurt their children. Taking responsibility for one's mistakes is a first step toward personal growth. Experiencing guilt can be useful when it motivates a person to change for the better, develop a plan to become the kind of person he or she wants to be, and put that plan into action. This process models what parents want their struggling teens to do too.

▲ Seek support and guidance for yourself in dealing with adolescence. Parents may feel embarrassed when their child is having trouble.

Parents of struggling teens often feel isolated from parents with "normal" teens. They may feel there is a conspiracy of silence: Why aren't other parents talking about their child's shoplifting charges, failing grades, recent abortion, or bout with gonorrhea? Parents may feel blamed, stigmatized, marginalized and silenced, and fearful of condemnation for having a child in trouble. Remember that millions of other parents of struggling teens are out there. Their silence separates them from each other. By talking to each other, parents of struggling teens can help one another.

▲ Do not despair. Adolescence is stormy for most families. Time, growth, and maturation can help.

Form a United Front

It is extremely helpful when the teen's parents are on the same page, forming a united front, asserting the same rules, expectations, and consequences. This is true when both parents are in the home, when there is divorce or separation, or with never-married parents or step-parents. All teenagers, not just those who act out and defy authority, can be masters at splitting parents and playing one off against the other. Teenagers who hear inconsistent or contradictory messages from parents are freer to follow their own destructive instincts, as in "My parents don't agree, so I may as well do what I want." Teenagers whose parents present a united front may give up trying to divide and conquer. It may sound simplistic, but there is considerable truth to the adage that two against one nearly always wins.

Most parents of struggling teens disagree with each other at least sometimes, perhaps often. The intense, emotional, frightening, and frustrating situations in their family breed disagreement. It is not unusual for one parent to lobby for "tough love" while the other pushes for a gentler approach. Both parents may have reasonable perspectives—both may be right! No wonder the argument goes round and round. Hot crises involving teenagers easily can lead to marital and relationship conflicts as parents make difficult decisions about rules, consequences, counseling, out-of-home placements, and so on. Frequent and ample opportunity for disagreement exists. Hence, parents of struggling teens need to be especially vigilant in their efforts to collaborate and develop a genuinely united front, for their child's sake and for the sake of the parents' relationship. Periodic consultation with a therapist or marriage counselor can help parents accomplish this unity.

Let Go and Hold On

Parents of children who have struggled for a long time have lots of experience stepping in to pick up the pieces. For instance, your six-year-old goes to school, accidentally leaving his or her lunch bag on the kitchen table and you drive the bag to school so your young child will not be hungry; when your 16-year-old does the same thing, it may be time to let your child experience the consequences of his forgetfulness. When your 17-year-old gets a speeding ticket, it is important that it be paid out of the teen's own savings.

"Letting go" does not mean abandoning one's child. The parent of a drug-using child can say, "You can't continue to steal from me. We can't go on like this. I've changed the locks on our front and back doors. You may call this telephone number and enroll in this drug treatment program. When you complete the program, you may return home. I love you too much to continue to enable your drug use." Holding on while letting go is a delicate balance that varies in each situation.

Letting go while hanging on may seem like a contradiction; it is not, particularly when parenting struggling teens. As everyone knows, adolescents are programmed to separate from parents as they move into adulthood. This is natural. Yet, struggling teens give parents every reason in the world to hold on to the leash for dear life, to maintain close supervision, and to avoid letting go. Conscientious, caring parents cannot let go precisely when their struggling children are most out of control and in need of close supervision to ensure safety.

The challenge for all parents of struggling teens is to find the right balance between letting go and hanging on. Hanging on too tightly can be counterproductive, particularly with teenagers who have rebellious instincts. Forceful parental supervision may be met by equally forceful rebellion. Also, the stark reality is that these teenagers are marching quickly toward the age of emancipation, when they will be legally responsible for their decisions and behaviors. Like watching one's toddler swim for the first time without a flotation device, parents of struggling teens must reach a point where they let go and hope for the best. If teenagers founder, parents can offer assistance but, before long, a teenager will be a young adult who must manage on his or her own. Parents need to work hard toward gradual and steady release while continuing to care and offer support in a constructive way. Figuring out this ever-shifting balance is an art.

Accept Painful Truths

Most people enter parenthood with dreams about having deeply satisfying, rewarding relationships with their children as they grow and develop successfully. When a teen begins to struggle, parents often view the descent as a reflection on their parenting abilities. After all, what makes a parent look perfect? A perfect child! The struggling teen can feel like an assault on a parent's dreams, abilities, and self-esteem. Many parents discover during their children's adolescence that the best-laid parenting plans sometimes turn into nightmares. The cute infant has become contentious and unmanageable.

One of life's great challenges is accepting painful truths. The unalterable truth may be that one's child has issues that are enormously frustrating to the child and you. Some features of people's personalities and behavior can be changed, but some cannot. Parents of struggling teens may need to abandon fantasies of the "ideal child" and learn how to accept, honor, and celebrate the real child they have. Parents who can grieve the loss of the fantasy child are freer to appreciate their actual child's charms and gifts while addressing the child's challenges.

Learn How to Cope with Shame and Isolation

Parents of struggling teens know the pain associated with unwelcome news that their child is in some kind of trouble. They are all too used to telephone calls from the school guidance counselor, teacher, vice principal, police, or summer camp director that begin with something like, "We need to talk—it seems we have a serious problem here with your child." Parents of struggling teens usually have a large collection of stories about their trips to school, the police station, or elsewhere for yet another meeting to talk about their child's mischief, distress, inappropriate behavior, or poor performance. Meeting after meeting is filled with hand wringing and earnest efforts to help the teen get back on track. Professionals and parents either lock horns or put their heads together in an attempt to provide the teen with useful supports, incentives, and appropriate sanctions.

In each instance parents may feel shame, disappointment, sadness, frustration, fear, and anger. Parents may wonder, "Why us?" particularly as they scan school hallways and friends' homes and see countless other teenagers who seem to be able to avoid these troubles "Why can't our kid be like all those other kids?" they think. Over time, parents of struggling teens may find it difficult to socialize with other parents whose children seem to skate through adolescence without any significant spill, win athletic trophies, star in school plays, volunteer in hospitals, achieve high scores on their SATs, and win admission to prestigious colleges and universities.

The reality, of course, is that most parents encounter rough spots—some deeper and wider than others—with their teenagers. Some parents whose children get into trouble feel so much shame that they find it hard to acknowledge their situation publicly and imagine that they are the only ones in such dire straits. Gradually they isolate themselves, perhaps limiting their social contact to a few select parents in similar circumstances.

Parents of struggling teens often find it helpful to acknowledge their "situation" with a few trustworthy, nonjudgmental friends, including friends whose teenagers are not struggling. Storing up and holding in one's pain and frustration can be debilitating and, ultimately, self-destructive. Sharing one's plight with sensitive and supportive friends can provide much-needed solace.

Obtain Emotional Support: Self-Care

Parents of struggling teens need to take care of themselves. A solo pilot flying through extremely turbulent weather is in a risky predicament; the pilot must be vigilant and alert, or the plane will crash. When exhaustion sets in, disaster is more likely. Living with intense stress without support or relief can seriously erode one's health and ability to cope with the next crisis.

Parents of struggling teens may show signs of severe stress, including the following typical symptoms:[2]

▲ Difficulty communicating thoughts

▲ Difficulty sleeping

---

2. Portions of this discussion are adapted from the National Mental Health Information Center, Center for Mental Health Services, Substance Abuse and Mental Health Services Administration, U.S. Department of Health and Human Services (available at http://www.mentalhealth.samhsa.gov/publications/allpubs/KEN-01-0097/default.asp).

▲ Becoming easily frustrated

▲ Increased use of drugs and alcohol

▲ Limited attention span

▲ Poor work performance

▲ Headaches or stomach problems

▲ Tunnel vision

▲ Colds or flulike symptoms

▲ Disorientation or confusion

▲ Difficulty concentrating

▲ Reluctance to leave home

▲ Depression or sadness

▲ Feelings of hopelessness

▲ Mood swings

▲ Crying easily

▲ Overwhelming guilt and self-doubt

▲ Fear of crowds, strangers, or being alone.

What can parents of a struggling teen do to care for themselves as they wend their way through their family crisis? Mental health professionals recommend a number of ways to ease stress:

▲ Talk with someone about your feelings—resentment, sorrow, and other emotions—even though it may be difficult. It is important to express your intense feelings so they do not eat away at you.

▲ Do not hold yourself solely responsible for your situation or berate yourself because you cannot fix the problem. Parents of struggling teens cannot perform miracles. All they can do is put one foot in front of the other as they go through the slow process of responding to crises, assessing risks, contacting professionals, and arranging services and interventions.

▲ Eat healthfully. Exercise daily. Get a full night's sleep. Try to relax. Find time for spiritual rejuvenation and reflection. This healthful lifestyle can help sustain you. Getting stressed out and run down will not improve the situation. Your teenager's life may be spinning out of control, but you do not have to go down, too.

▲ Limit unnecessary demands and responsibilities on yourself and your family. Maintain a normal daily routine; your hands are full enough. Routine can help you avoid getting lost in the chaos that surrounds many struggling teens.

▲ Spend time with supportive family and friends. Emotional support is healing and critical during stressful times. Do your best to maintain a healthy social life to avoid isolation.

Think Beyond the Crisis: The Long View

Understandably, parents of struggling teens often are preoccupied with immediate crises. When teens spin out of control at home, in school, or in the community, parents need to respond quickly: Do we intervene this time or do we let our child go under and experience the consequences, so she or he learns a lesson? Of course, in the face of crises, it can be hard to take the long view and appreciate how complex and slow the process of change can be. In the heat of the moment, parents may feel intense pressure to figure out immediately how to get their child reinstated in school following a suspension, bailed out of a juvenile detention facility, admitted to a substance abuse treatment program or residential treatment center, or transported to a remotely located wilderness therapy program.

It may help, however, for parents to realize that the change process often is more like a marathon than a sprint. Over time—usually considerable time—many struggling teens make significant progress, especially if their parents and the professionals in their lives are able to locate constructive and effective services, programs, and schools. The pace of progress varies tremendously among teens; some move in the right direction more quickly than others. For some teens, the path is filled with fits and starts and quite a few speed bumps and detours. For others, the path is more linear and smooth. Wise parents realize that much of what happens on that path is out of their control; they simply do the best they can to provide the right supports and environment to enable their child to progress as much and as quickly as possible.

Parents of struggling teens sometime hope for the miracle "cure." They hope that the very next therapist, school, or program will be just what the doctor ordered and will fix the problem. Realistically, however, we know that teenagers facing serious emotional, behavioral, social, and academic challenges often require years to experience significant change.

Part of the challenge is to provide the right kind of scaffolding and support to struggling teens while their brains mature, particularly the frontal lobe, which is responsible for the ability to learn from consequences and *executive function*, a cluster of high-order capacities that are especially important during adolescence and include selective attention, behavioral planning and impulse control, and the manipulation of information in problem-solving tasks. Adolescents whose brains are not fully developed and have difficulty with executive function are more likely to experience emotional difficulties (for example, aggression, mood swings, suicidal ideation), risk-taking and impulsive behaviors (for example, alcohol and drug use, unprotected sex), attention problems (for example, distractibility, poor academic planning), and compulsive behaviors (for example, alcohol and drug abuse, self-mutilation, eating disorders, preoccupation with appearance). Thus, an important task with struggling teens is to place them in protected, supervised settings that can contain their inappropriate, impulsive, destructive, and counterproductive behaviors, keeping them safe during this critical period of brain development. As the brain matures, many struggling teens show evidence of improved judgment, better impulse control, more stable moods, and more appropriate behavior. Clearly, patience—a great deal of patience—is a virtue for parents of struggling teens. Keeping one eye on the long-range plan while the other eye is focused on the immediate crisis may help parents weather the acute and chronic storms.

CHAPTER 5

Helpful Resources:

WHERE CAN WE GET MORE INFORMATION?

Information about services and programs for struggling teens and families is available from social workers, schools, public child welfare agencies, juvenile and family courts, family service agencies, community mental health centers, educational advocates, educational consultants, clergy, and lawyers. Valuable information is available on Web sites and various directories and publications. Below is a list of key resources:

▲ For information about family service agencies that provide assistance to struggling teens and their families (including a directory of programs):

- The Alliance for Children and Families (http://www.alliance1. org/) is a national membership association of private, nonprofit child- and family-serving agencies.

▲ For information about substance abuse and mental health treatment programs:

- The Mental Health Services Locator, Center for Mental Health Services, Substance Abuse and Mental Health Services Administration (SAMHSA), U.S. Department of Health and Human Services (http://www.mentalhealth.samhsa.gov/databases/) enables parents to locate mental health services throughout the United States.

- The Substance Abuse Treatment Facility Locator, Center for Substance Abuse Treatment, Substance Abuse and Mental Health Services Administration, U.S. Department of Health and Human Services (http://findtreatment.samhsa.gov/) enables parents to locate substance abuse treatment facilities throughout the United States.

- The Commission on Accreditation of Rehabilitation Facilities (CARF) (http://www.carf.org/) accredits alcohol and substance abuse treatment programs; child and youth service programs; mental health and behavioral health programs; and supported living programs. The CARF Web site enables parents to search for accredited programs throughout the United States.

- The Council on Accreditation (COA) (www.coanet.org) accredits organizations that provide community-based and residential services such as alcohol and chemical dependency counseling; case management; supported and independent living; individual and family counseling; and day treatment. The COA Web site enables parents to search for accredited programs throughout the United States and Canada.

- The Joint Commission on Accreditation of Healthcare Organizations (JCAHO) (http://www.jcaho.org/) accredits a wide range of health care organizations, including behavioral health programs that serve struggling teens. The JCAHO Web site enables parents to search for accredited programs throughout the United States.

▲ For information about mentoring programs for teenagers:

- The MENTOR/National Mentoring Partnership (http://www.mentoring.org/) is a national organization that works with state and local mentoring programs to serve youths. MENTOR provides a directory of mentoring programs and partnerships.

▲ For information about alternative high schools, emotional-growth boarding schools, therapeutic boarding schools, and residential treatment centers:

- The Coalition of Essential Schools (CES) (http://www.essentialschools.org/) was created in 1984 by a group of 12 schools in seven states in an effort to reform education in the United States. Currently the CES network includes approximately 600 schools. These schools base their teaching and curriculum on a series of core common principles—grounded in theory and extensive research—that are particularly well suited for struggling teens who are more likely to thrive in nontraditional school settings where they receive personalized instruction to address their individual needs and interests.

- The Association of Boarding Schools (TABS) (http://www.schools.com/) is a voluntary membership organization for boarding schools in the United States, Canada, and abroad. This nonprofit organization maintains comprehensive listings and a directory of information about specialty boarding schools. The TABS Web site enables parents to search for boarding schools.

- National Association of Therapeutic Schools and Programs (NATSAP) (http://www.natsap.org/) is a national membership organization for therapeutic schools, residential treatment centers, wilderness therapy programs, transitional living programs, young adult programs, and home-based residential programs. The NATSAP Web site enables parents to search for schools and programs throughout the United States.

- Woodbury Reports sponsors the Struggling Teens Web site (http://www.strugglingteens.com/), which provides valuable information to parents, including information about schools and programs, an online discussion forum, newsletter, resource listings, and parent reviews of schools and programs. (Parents should be aware that this Web site accepts paid advertisements from schools and programs, although inclusion on the Web site does not imply endorsement by Woodbury Reports.)

▲ For information about helping children with ADHD:

- Children and Adults with Attention-Deficit/Hyperactivity Disorder (CHADD) (http://www.chadd.org/) is a nonprofit organization serving people with ADHD and their families. CHADD sponsors chapters throughout the United States. Chapters offer support for individuals, parents, teachers, professionals, and others. CHADD also provides contact information for educational advocates, educational consultants, coaches, and mental health providers.

▲ For information about 12-step groups for teenagers with addictions:

- Alcoholics Anonymous (http://www.alcoholics-anonymous. org/), or AA, is a well-known 12-step program. AA is the model on which all other 12-step programs are based. Participants in this voluntary fellowship share their experiences with one another in an effort to attain and maintain sobriety. AA is a program of total abstinence. Sobriety is maintained through sharing experiences at group meetings and through the program's 12 steps for recovery from alcoholism.

- Cocaine Anonymous (CA) (http://www.ca.org/) is a voluntary 12-step fellowship program in which participants share their experiences with one another in an effort to attain and maintain a drug-free lifestyle. CA is a program of total abstinence. Abstinence is maintained through sharing experiences at group meetings and through the program's 12 steps for recovery from cocaine addiction.

- Narcotics Anonymous (NA) (http://www.na.org/) is a voluntary 12-step fellowship program in which participants share their experiences with one another in an effort to attain and maintain abstinence. NA is a program of total abstinence. Abstinence is maintained through sharing experiences at group meetings and through the program's 12 steps for recovery from narcotics addiction.

- Gamblers Anonymous (GA) (http://www.gamblersanonymous.org/) is a voluntary 12-step fellowship program in which participants share their experiences with one another in an effort to stop compulsive gambling. GA is a program of total abstinence. Recovery is maintained through sharing experiences at group meetings and through the program's 12 steps for recovery from compulsive gambling.

- Food Addicts Anonymous (FA) (http://www.foodaddictsanonymous.org/) is a voluntary 12-step fellowship program in which participants share their experiences with one another in an effort to deal with food addiction. Recovery is maintained through sharing experiences at group meetings and through the program's 12 steps for recovery from food addiction.

- Overeaters Anonymous (OA) (http://www.oa.org/index.htm) is a voluntary 12-step fellowship program in which participants share their experiences with one another in an effort to deal with food addiction. Recovery is maintained through sharing experiences at group meetings and through the program's 12 steps for recovery from food addiction.

▲ For information about wilderness therapy programs:

- Wilderness Therapy and Outdoor Behavioral Health Treatment Programs (http://www.wilderness-therapy.org/) provides comprehensive information about wilderness therapy programs on its Web site. Parents will find useful articles about the nature and goals of wilderness therapy programs; how to find safe and effective programs; program descriptions; feedback from parents whose children have participated in these programs; risk assessment and screening questionnaires; and clinical, health, and safety issues in wilderness therapy programs.

▲ For information about specialty courts for teenagers:

- National Youth Court Center (http://www.youthcourt.net/), sponsored by the National Association of Probation and Parole, provides an updated list of specialty courts throughout the United States.

▲ For information about independent living programs for teenagers:

- National Independent Living Association (NILA) (http://www.nilausa.org/) provides a national network for providing information about independent living programs. The NILA Web site includes a list of member agencies throughout the United States.

▲ For information about independent educational consultants:

- Independent Educational Consultants Association (IECA) (http://www.educationalconsulting.org/) is a nonprofit professional association of full-time, experienced educational consultants. IECA maintains an updated Internet directory of educational consultants and can help parents find a consultant with expertise related to the teenager's unique needs.

▲ For information about financial aid and loans:

- The eStudentLoan Web site (http://www.estudentloan.com/) provides parents with detailed information about various financial aid and student loan options.

- The prepGATE Web site (http://www.prepgate.com/) provides parents with information about long-term loans to pay for specialty schools and programs.

Several books and publications may be helpful to parents:

▲ Gary Ferguson, *Shouting at the Sky: Troubled Teens and the Promise of the Wild* (New York: St. Martins Press, 1999). Ferguson is a writer who spent time traveling with a group of teenagers participating in the Aspen Achievement Academy's wilderness therapy program. This book provides parents with a realistic glimpse of this unique treatment approach.

▲ David L. Marcus, *What It Takes To Pull Me Through: Why Teenagers Get In Trouble and How Four of Them Got Out* (New York: Houghton Mifflin, 2005). Marcus writes about the lives of teens enrolled at the Academy at Swift River, a therapeutic boarding school in Massachusetts. The book provides a realistic look at a highly structured program for struggling teens.

▲ Carol Maxym and Leslie York, *Teens in Turmoil: A Path to Change for Parents, Adolescents, and Their Families* (New York: Penguin Books, 2001). This book, by a psychotherapist and educational consultant, discusses the nature of struggling teens and the range of options and resources available to parents.

▲ Scott P. Sells, *Parenting Your Out of Control Teenager* (New York: St. Martins Press, 2002). This book by a family therapist provides useful insights and advice about parenting a struggling teen.

▲ Ron Taffel, *Breaking Through to Teens: A New Psychotherapy for the New Adolescence* (New York: Guilford Press, 2005). Taffel, a psychologist, provides an insightful analysis of the challenges facing contemporary adolescents and their parents.

▲ Woodbury Reports, *The Parent Empowerment Handbook*. This guide, updated periodically, provides detailed summaries of programs and schools for struggling teens. In addition to program descriptions, this publication includes advice columns, essays, and articles on various issues facing parents. This guide can be ordered through the Struggling Teens Web site: http://www.strugglingteens. com/

CHAPTER **6**

Financial Issues:

HOW DO WE PAY FOR THIS?

Programs and services for struggling teens can be expensive. Some families have health insurance that pays for all or part of programs that provide mental health treatment. The teenager's public school system may pay all or part of the cost, or a court may require the public child welfare agency to pay. Unfortunately, a public school system, child welfare agency, or juvenile court may insist on substantial evidence of a teen's long, deep slide into drug addiction, school failure, pregnancy, and criminal justice entanglement before agreeing to pay for specialty programs or schools. In the meantime, a juvenile court judge may send an out-of-control child to the state or county juvenile detention facility, not a treatment program. If parents wait while the child continues to spin out of control, serious harm may result (for example, HIV infection, drug addiction, pregnancy, incarceration). Some parents are unwilling to take that risk and arrange to pay for services and programs themselves; others have no choice but to wait for formal approval and government subsidies from school departments and public child welfare agencies.

Affluent families may be able to pay for programs and services "out of pocket," but many families cannot afford needed programs and services, do not have adequate insurance, and are unable to obtain funding from their public school department or public child welfare agency. In some instances, parents who cannot afford needed services agree to give legal custody of their teen to the local public child welfare agency, which then funds the services or programs (in several states, the public child welfare agency will fund services without requiring that parents hand over legal custody). In still other circumstances, desperate parents may turn to the juvenile or family court and formally request that the teen be declared "wayward," thus enabling the court to require the child to accept intervention. In those cases the state typically pays for needed services and programs. Some parents may be reluctant to use this route to services because then the court, not they, determine where the child goes for help.

Some communities have multiservice agencies committed to helping low-income struggling teens and their families. Those programs may be funded by state and local government agencies, school districts, foundations, or the United Way. The agencies provide services to struggling teens and their families free of charge or for reduced fees. Low-income families of struggling teens may be able to find these programs by asking state or local child welfare officials, school personnel, and social service providers affiliated with the local juvenile or family court.[1]

Many private programs—wilderness therapy programs, emotional-growth boarding schools, therapeutic boarding schools, and residential treatment centers—will help parents apply for low-interest loans. Private loan programs, such as prepGATE (http://www.prepgate.com/) and eStudentLoan (http://www.estudentloan.com/), also provide parents with various financing options. Some private programs offer a limited number of scholarships for teens from low-income families.

---

1. A good example of this kind of multiservice agency is Tides Family Services , which provides comprehensive care for at-risk teens in economically distressed Rhode Island communities. About 85 percent of Tides' clients live below the poverty line; approximately 60 percent are teens of color. Most of the program's teens have been labeled "wayward" or out of control by the local family court. Many have been adjudicated for delinquent behavior. Tides' programs are paid for by a variety of contracts with public and private agencies; school departments; and grants from foundations, banks, and religious and other organizations. The agency provides a wide range of services and programs, including Tides Learning Center, an alternative school for struggling teens that includes after-school activities to enhance learning and social skills; Youth New Futures (intensive supervision for youths returning home from the state juvenile correctional facility and youths on probation); Home-based Therapeutic Services, (intensive home-based and community-based services to teens who have severe behavioral, emotional, and psychiatric challenges); Outreach and Tracking Program (intensive face-to-face outreach to teens involved with the juvenile justice and child welfare systems); Youth Diversion Program (an early intervention program for teens showing signs of distress but not yet involved in the juvenile justice system); and the Latino Outreach Project (a social service and counseling program designed to provide bilingual services to Latino teens and their families, including individual, family, and group counseling; parent support groups; educational advocacy; family court advocacy; and sex offender and victim counseling).

Some families show remarkable resourcefulness and creativity in generating funds for specialty programs and schools. They may draw on college savings, concluding that a teen who does not survive or complete high school will never make it to college and that now is the time to spend the money to increase the chances that the teen will have a brighter future. Some families also refinance their home or draw on retirement savings. Some families are fortunate to have relatives who are willing to help out financially.

Index

Postscript

Parents of struggling teens have their hands full. Although all parents of struggling teens have moments of despair, an impressive array of professionals and resources can, indeed, make an enormous difference. For many teens, quick fixes are not realistic; steady, persistent, compassionate, and purposeful interventions are possible and, often, are effective.

Parenting a struggling teenager is among life's greatest challenges. Making a positive, significant difference in a struggling teenager's life is among the most rewarding experiences any parent can have.

About the Authors

Frederic G. Reamer, PhD, is professor in the graduate program of the School of Social Work, Rhode Island College. His research and teaching have addressed a wide range of human service issues, including mental health, health care, criminal justice public welfare, and professional ethics. Dr. Reamer has served as a social worker in correctional and mental health settings and has lectured extensively nationally and internationally on the subjects of professional ethics and professional malpractice and liability. Dr. Reamer received the Distinguished Contributions to Social Work Education award from the Council on Social Education (1995) and the Presidential Award from National Association of Social Workers (1997).

Dr. Reamer's books include *Heinous Crime: Cases, Causes, and Consequences* (Columbia University Press); *Pocket Guide to Essential Human Services* (NASW Press); *Criminal Lessons: Case Studies and Commentary on Crime and Justice* (Columbia University Press); *Social Work Values and Ethics* (Columbia University Press); *Tangled Relationships: Managing Boundary Issues in the Human Services* (Columbia University Press); *Ethical Standards in Social Work: A Review of the NASW Code of Ethics* (NASW Press); *The Social Work Ethics Audit: A Risk Management Tool* (NASW Press); *Ethics Education in Social Work* (Council on Social Work Education); *The Foundations of Social Work Knowledge* (Columbia University Press; editor and contributor); *Social Work Malpractice and Liability* (Columbia University Press); *Social Work Research and Evaluation Skills* (Columbia University Press); *The Philosophical Foundations of Social Work* (Columbia University Press); *AIDS and Ethics* (Columbia University Press; editor and contributor); *Ethical Dilemmas in Social Service* (Columbia University Press); *Rehabilitating Juvenile Justice* (Columbia University Press; coauthor, Charles H. Shireman); *The Teaching of Social Work Ethics* (The Hastings Center; coauthor, Marcia Abramson).

Deborah H. Siegel, PhD, LICSW, DCSW, ACSW, is a social work practitioner, researcher, and educator. She is professor in the graduate program of the School of Social Work, Rhode Island College, where she has been on the faculty since 1983. She served as an Edith Abbott Research and Teaching Fellow at the University of Chicago, School of Social Service Administration, and as a faculty member and director of field instruction in the Department of Sociology,

Anthropology, and Social Work at Auburn University, and at the University of Missouri-Columbia, School of Social Work. Her clinical work specializes in families with children and teens who struggle at school, at home, and in the community. Dr. Siegel's research and publications in professional journals address clinical practice evaluation, adoption issues, and attention deficit hyperactivity disorder. Her current research explores how open adoptions (those in which biological and adoptive families have contact with each other) evolve over time. Professor Siegel is a frequent presenter at adoption work-shops and conferences and is a consultant for adoption agencies.